The Word Weavers

Modern journalism is often the subject of criticism and opposition. Written by a leading authority on language and the media, this engaging book suggests that view is unfair, and that journalists are in fact skilled 'word weavers' whose output is cleverly worked into planned patterns. Drawing on a range of authentic news articles, the book traces the development of journalism from its origins to the present day. Aitchison shows how contemporary news writers have inherited an age-old oral tradition, which over the centuries was incorporated into public notices, ballads and newsbooks – eventually providing the basis of the journalism we see today. She argues that, while journalists have very different aims from literary writers, their work can in no way be regarded as inferior. Entertainingly written, *The Word Weavers* provides a fascinating insight into journalistic writing, and will be enjoyed by anybody wanting to know more about media language.

JEAN AITCHISON is Emeritus Rupert Murdoch Professor of Language and Communication, Worcester College, University of Oxford. Her previous books include *The Language Web: The Power and Problem of Words* (1997), *Language Change: Progress or Decay?* (3rd edition 2003) and *The Seeds of Speech: Language Origin and Evolution* (Canto edition 2000), all published by Cambridge University Press.

The Word Weavers

Newshounds and Wordsmiths

Jean Aitchison

Emeritus Rupert Murdoch Professor of Language and Communication, University of Oxford

CAMBRIDGE
UNIVERSITY PRESS

CAMBRIDGE UNIVERSITY PRESS
Cambridge, New York, Melbourne, Madrid, Cape Town, Singapore, São Paulo

Cambridge University Press
The Edinburgh Building, Cambridge CB2 8RU, UK

Published in the United States of America by Cambridge University Press,
New York

www.cambridge.org
Information on this title: www.cambridge.org/9780521540070

First published 2007

Printed in the United Kingdom at the University Press, Cambridge

A catalogue record for this publication is available from the British Library

Library of Congress Cataloguing in Publication data

Aitchison, Jean, 1938–
The word weavers : newshounds and wordsmiths / Jean Aitchison.
    p. cm. – (Cambridge approaches to linguistics)
Includes bibliographical references and index.
ISBN-13 978-0-521-83245-8 (hardback : alk. paper)
ISBN-10 0-521-83245-4 (hardback : alk. paper)
ISBN-13 978-0-521-54007-0 (pbk. : alk. paper)
ISBN-10 0-521-54007-0 (pbk. : alk. paper)
1. Journalism and literature. 2. Journalism–Technique. I. Title. II. Series.
PN4759.A48   2007
808'.06607–dc22   2006036799

ISBN 978-0-521-83245-8 hardback
ISBN 978-0-521-54007-0 paperback

Shooting the messenger

The street seller of newspapers
is growing old.
One glance and you can tell
that a lifetime of violence
has taken its toll.

War and murder have been
meat and drink to him.
Think of all the catastrophic news
of which he has been the bearer,
all the sensational headlines

he has put through his hands,
all the scandal he has spread,
all the famous dead of whom
his tabloids have spoken badly.
At day's end, when he checks

how many papers are left,
he counts them pensively,
as if preparing a defence,
as if each were a year for which
he simply cannot account.

DENNIS O'DRISCOLL

CONTENTS

FIGURES

PREFACE

The word weavers is a book about newshounds
(journalists) and wordsmiths (literary writers). Both
of them are skilled word weavers, whose output is
consciously woven into patterns, unlike most of the
words spontaneously uttered in everyday speech.

Humans, alone among apes, have a bizarre extra
ability. They open and shut their mouths and utter
strange, complex noises which their fellow humans
understand. In short, they are born to use language.
For tens of thousands of years this linguistic talent was
purely oral. Humans gossiped, persuaded, informed
and entertained one another by word of mouth. These
centuries of oral tradition have largely been forgotten.
Yet they had an indelible effect on current-day media
and literature. Luckily, we can peel away some of the
relatively recent layers and reveal a hidden oral core,
which had a huge influence on later written output.

Our own early oral tradition is revealed in sage
saws and old ballads. These in turn were incorporated
into broadsides, chapbooks and newsbooks and,
eventually, into modern journalism. A later literary

tradition undervalued these old roots, and (wrongly) proclaimed itself to be superior. This book explores this old rivalry. It shows that the media need to be properly evaluated, and reinstated in their rightful place as parallel to, and in no way inferior to, conventional English literature.

As always, I am enormously grateful to the numerous people who have helped in the emergence of this book. First of all, my thanks go to News International who funded my Chair at Oxford University, the Rupert Murdoch Professorship of Language and Communication, of which I was the first holder. This was a challenging and enjoyable post. All my life I have eagerly gobbled up media output, so it was a privilege to be paid to read and analyse newspapers, and other media, a pastime that I had previously regarded as a spare-time activity. Secondly, my thanks go to the Faculty of English at Oxford, to both students and staff. The English Faculty students who chose to do the final-year option on language and the media undoubtedly sharpened my thoughts on the topic with their challenging questions and thought-provoking essays. I am also grateful for the support I received from numerous members of staff, especially my research assistant Diana Lewis, and colleagues Ros Ballaster, Lynda Mugglestone and John Carey. Thanks also to Worcester College, Oxford, (the old college of Rupert Murdoch) which provided me with colleagues to whom I enjoyed chatting, and an office which was a pleasure to work in: it looked out onto trees and a lake. Numerous others (too many to mention) have helped me in the ten years I was at Oxford. Their

valuable aid is tucked into several sections of this
book: they have provided references, suggested interesting angles, and discussed controversial topics. Staff
at News International were also generous with their
time, especially Jane Reed. Chris Whalley and Richard
Bonfield helped me with illustrations involving newspapers. Andrew Winnard, Helen Barton, Elizabeth
Davey and Leigh Mueller at Cambridge University
Press deserve my thanks for the efficiency with which
the book has been produced. Finally, I thank my
husband, the lexicographer John Ayto, who sustains
me endlessly with encouraging words, non-stop loving
kindness, and mouth-watering meals.

JEAN AITCHISON

ACKNOWLEDGEMENTS

The publishers gratefully acknowledge the help of the many organizations in collecting the illustrations and text extracts for this volume. Every effort has been made to obtain permission to use copyright materials; the publishers apologize for any omissions and would welcome these being brought to their attention.

Text extracts

p. v Poem 'Shooting the messenger' by Dennis O'Driscoll. Reproduced with the kind permission of Anvil Press Poetry and the *Oxford Magazine*

p. 122 Evans 2000:75. 'Edward the donkey' from *Essential English for journalists, editors and writers*. Reproduced with the kind permission of The Random House Group Ltd

p. 149 R. S. Thomas b. 1913. Four lines from 'Don't ask me', Thomas 2000:69. Reproduced with the kind permission of Bloodaxe Books Ltd

p. 158 R. S. Thomas. Ten lines from 'Vocabulary', Thomas 2000:63. Reproduced with the kind permission of Bloodaxe Books Ltd

p. 150 William Carlos Williams d. 1963. Poem 'From a play' (sixteen lines, 1942), from Williams 1988:44–5. Reproduced with the kind permission of Bloodaxe Books Ltd

p. 150 Richard Wilbur, poem 'Opposites', lines 1–4, in Wilbur 2005. Reproduced with the kind permission of Harcourt Brace

Images

Figure 1.1 Condemnation of newspapers, reproduced with the kind permission of the Bodleian library

Figure 3.1 Clay tokens, from David Crystal, *The Cambridge Encyclopedia of Language, Second Edition*, p. 198, reproduced with the kind permission of Cambridge University Press

Figure 4.1 Robin O'Green of Burnley, in O'Connell 1999:2, 253, reproduced with the kind permission of the British Museum

Figure 4.2 'A Proper newe Ballad', *Society's Broadside*, in O'Connell 1989:90, reproduced with the kind permission of the Society of Antiquaries

Figure 4.3 A PERFECT DIURNAL OF THE PASSAGES In Parliament (Raymond 1993:474), reproduced with the kind permission of the Bodleian library

Figure 5.1 Souvenir edition of *The Times*, 6 November 1805, reproduced with the kind permission of News International

Figure 5.2 Funeral of Nelson, *The Times*, 10 November 1805, reproduced with the kind permission of News International

Figure 6.2 ANOTHER MURDER IN WHITECHAPEL, *The Times*, 1 September 1888, reproduced with the kind permission of News International

Figure 7.1 GOTCHA. *Sun*, 4 May 1982, reproduced with the kind permission of News International

Figure 7.2 'Denise is Totty with Top Botty', *Sun*, 22 October 1999, reproduced with the kind permission of News International

Figure 9.1 Birdiness rankings, from Aitchison 2003b:56, reproduced with the kind permission of Blackwell Publishing Ltd

CHAPTER ONE

Weaving and worrying

Journalism versus literature?

> I was up all night worrying about myself and my connection
> to language.   Irwin Shaw, *Beggarman, thief* (1977)[1]

'What's a Nupiter Piffkin?', 'Don't be frightened of
banshees', 'Henry VIII had six wives', 'Helen wants to
film a salamander', 'Look at that dragonish cloud',
are all possible English sentences.

Yet a Nupiter Piffkin is a figment of a comic poet's
imagination:

> Mr and Mrs Discobolos
> Climbed to the top of a wall,
> And they sat to watch the sunset sky
> And to hear the Nupiter Piffkin cry
> And the Biscuit Buffalo call.[2]

A banshee is a fabled mythical creature, 'less a
shape than a mournful screaming that haunts the
Irish night', according to Jorge Luis Borges.[3] Henry
VIII's marriages took place several centuries ago,

1

Helen's film-making is in the future, and dragonish clouds exist only in the eyes and mind of a beholder, as in Shakespeare's play *Antony and Cleopatra*:

> Sometimes we see a cloud that's dragonish;
> A vapour sometime like a bear or lion,
> A towered citadel, a pendant rock,
> A forked mountain, or blue promontory
> With trees upon't.[4]

Humans use language in multiple ways and for many different reasons, as the examples above show. We can, of course, communicate by various other means: we can wave, wink, point, tap someone on the shoulder, and so on. But these other routes have not been fully exploited. A cheery wave or kiss on the cheek might help to cement a friendship, but could not convey detailed information. For that, language is required.

Our own act

Language develops 'naturally' in humans: 'The *natural disposition* to language is universal in man, and everyone must possess the key to the understanding of all languages', said the philosopher–linguist Wilhelm von Humboldt in 1836.[5] 'Man does not live on bread alone: his other necessity is communication', said the linguist Charles Hockett.[6] 'In nature's talent show we are simply a species with our own act, a knack for communicating who did what to whom by modulating the sounds we make when we exhale', wrote the psychologist Steven Pinker.[7]

Any human can learn any human language, and every human child has an overpowering urge to pick up any language he or she is exposed to at a young age.

The strong urge for humans to use language has a useful spin-off. It can be transferred from one medium to another: speech, sign or writing can all express the same message. If the spoken pathway is blocked, the need to develop language is so strong that an alternative is seized on by a child. As Ferdinand de Saussure, one of the 'fathers' of modern linguistics, said in 1915: 'What is natural to mankind is not spoken language but the faculty of constructing a language.'[8]

Language began in Africa, though exactly where is a matter of controversy. East Africa was the birthplace, according to a scenario sometimes known as the 'East Side story'.[9] Around 3 million years ago, a major earthquake created the Great Rift Valley, splitting Africa's inhabitants into two major groups. Our cousins, the chimps, were left living and playing in the lush and tree-rich terrain of the humid west. But our ancestors, the proto-humans, were stranded in the increasingly arid east, where they were forced to adapt or die. They came down from the few trees that were left in East Africa's dry savannah, and began to walk upright. They were forced to broaden their diet, and began scavenging for meat. Better nourishment led to a bigger brain, a greater degree of social organization and, eventually, to language.

But more important than the exact location of language within Africa is the fact that all human languages are remarkably similar to one another, indicating a common origin. Any human can learn any other human language. This contrasts with, say, bird communication, where the quacking of a duck has little in common with the trilling of a nightingale.

A primitive form of human language was probably in use from around 75,000 BP (before the present), perhaps even earlier.[10] It was almost certainly spoken, not signed or written. This proto-language had relatively few words, and minimal grammar. Full spoken language was firmly established before 50,000 BP. Archaeological evidence guarantees this. Waves of humans, with a culture superior to that of previous groups, emigrated out of Africa, into the Middle East, then travelled westward across Europe. Others went eastward to India and the Far East.[11]

Open-endedness

Humans perpetually juggle words, stringing them together in new and inventive ways. This talent has various labels: 'open-endedness' is perhaps the clearest, though 'creativity' and 'productivity' are also found.

The free range of human language contrasts with the output of most, perhaps all other animals, who can communicate about a limited set of topics only. In his 'Ode to a nightingale', the poet John Keats envies the nightingale:

> . . . thou, light-winged Dryad of the trees,
>   In some melodious plot
> Of beechen green, and shadows numberless,
> Singest of summer in full-throated ease.[12]

Yet birds are restricted in what they can warble about. Keats's nightingale was more likely enticing a mate, or warning others off its territory, than rhapsodizing about the season: most avian trills are about mating or territorial rights.[13]

Dolphins, via their echo-locating 'clicks', can distinguish between objects so similar that humans would judge them equal. Yet even dolphins are limited in what they can communicate about: distances and sizes are the main topic of dolphin 'conversation'.[14]

The ability to respond freely is another key aspect of creativity: no human is obliged to make a fixed response to any situation. People can say whatever they want, or even stay silent. If you were offered a large slice of cake, you might reply, 'Yes please'. But you could also have said, 'No, thank you, I'm slimming', or 'That looks marvellous! You must give me the recipe' or even 'Is that really a cake? It looks like a cow-pat.' Or you might have been so busy grabbing and chewing the cake that no reply was needed. Having a limitless range of possible responses is known (technically) as 'freedom from stimulus control'.

Many animals, on the other hand, make a fixed response to a certain stimulus. Chimps find it difficult to hold back excited 'yummy food' noises if they see something which whets their appetite: Figan, a young chimp who was given some bananas, made such delighted 'food, food' grunts that other chimps arrived, and grabbed his bananas – though he later learned to largely suppress these natural sounds, and was able to scoff his bananas in private.[15]

Instinctive grammarians

The open-endedness of language has another, less obvious aspect. Humans are instinctive grammarians, in that they can think and talk and write about language itself, as when the comic poet Ogden Nash contemplates a new word he's discovered:

> Seated one day at the dictionary I was pretty weary and also pretty ill at ease,
> Because a word I had always liked turned out not to be a word at all, and suddenly I found myself among the v's.
> And suddenly among the v's I came across a new word which was a word called *velleity*.
> So the new word I found was better than the old word I lost.[16]

This ability to contemplate language, and talk about it, contrasts with spiders, which cannot stand back and admire their handiwork. All humans, even young children, 'know something about language that the spider does not know about web-weaving':[17] 'Normally developing children not only become efficient users of language, they also spontaneously become little grammarians. By contrast, spiders, ants, beavers, and probably even chimpanzees do not have the potential to analyze their own knowledge.'[18]

A useful spin-off of this ability to think about language is the further skill of weaving it into conscious creative patterns. The poet Elizabeth Jennings pictures the process of composing poetry in her poem 'The house of words':

> It is a house you visit but don't stay
> For long. Words leap from ledges. Verbs and nouns
> Ask for a sentence where they'll fit and say

What you were unaware you thought. A dance
Of meanings happens in your head.[19]

More famously, a poet's 'intolerable wrestle / With
words and their meanings'[20] has been described by
T. S. Eliot:

Words strain,
Crack and sometimes break, under the burden,
Under the tension, slip, slide, perish,
Decay with imprecision, will not stay in place,
Will not stay still.[21]

Journalists also skilfully twist words into novel
patterns, though they are usually rushing to meet
deadlines: 'Journalism is literature in a hurry', is
a saying attributed to Matthew Arnold.[22]

Poetry praise, media moans

Yet these two types of word weavers, literary
writers (wordsmiths) and journalists (newshounds),
meet with different public reactions. The former are
typically highly rated: 'Great literature is simply language charged with meaning to the utmost possible
degree', said Ezra Pound in 1931.[23] Poetry, in particular, tends to be extravagantly praised: 'It [poetry]
is a species of painting with words, in which the
figures are happily conceived, ingeniously arranged,
affectingly expressed, and recommended with all the
warmth and harmony of colouring', asserted Oliver
Goldsmith in the eighteenth century.[24]

Meanwhile, the media often face fierce criticism.
Moans have bubbled up for centuries. Newsbooks, the

seventeenth-century forerunners of today's newspapers, were frequently condemned:

> For all those persons, that to tell,
>   And write much Newes do love,
> May Charon ferry them to hell,
>   And may they ne're remove,

ran a verse printed in the newsbook *Mercurius Anti-Mercurius*, in April 1648 (Fig. 1.1).[25]

The following spluttering condemnation by the fictional character, Sir Fretful Plagiary, in Richard Brinsley Sheridan's play *The Critic* (1779) reveals a long-standing, though often unexamined, dislike of the press: 'The newspapers! Sir, they are the most villainous – licentious – abominable – infernal – Not that I ever read them – No –, I make it a rule never to look into a newspaper.'[26] In the early nineteenth century, Samuel Coleridge asserted: 'The habit of perusing periodical works may be properly added to Averroes' catalogue of Anti-mnemonics, or weakeners of memory (which included eating of unripe fruit, gazing on clouds, riding among a multitude of camels, frequent laughter, and reading of tombstones in churchyards).'[27]

Such moans continued. Journalism is 'the vilest and most degrading of all trades' claimed the respected philosopher and economist John Stuart Mill, writing in the nineteenth century.[28] Similar caustic comments were made by numerous others: 'Among writers, those who do the most mischief are the original fabricators of error, to wit: the men generally who write for the newspapers',[29] wrote Edward Gould, in 1867. 'The

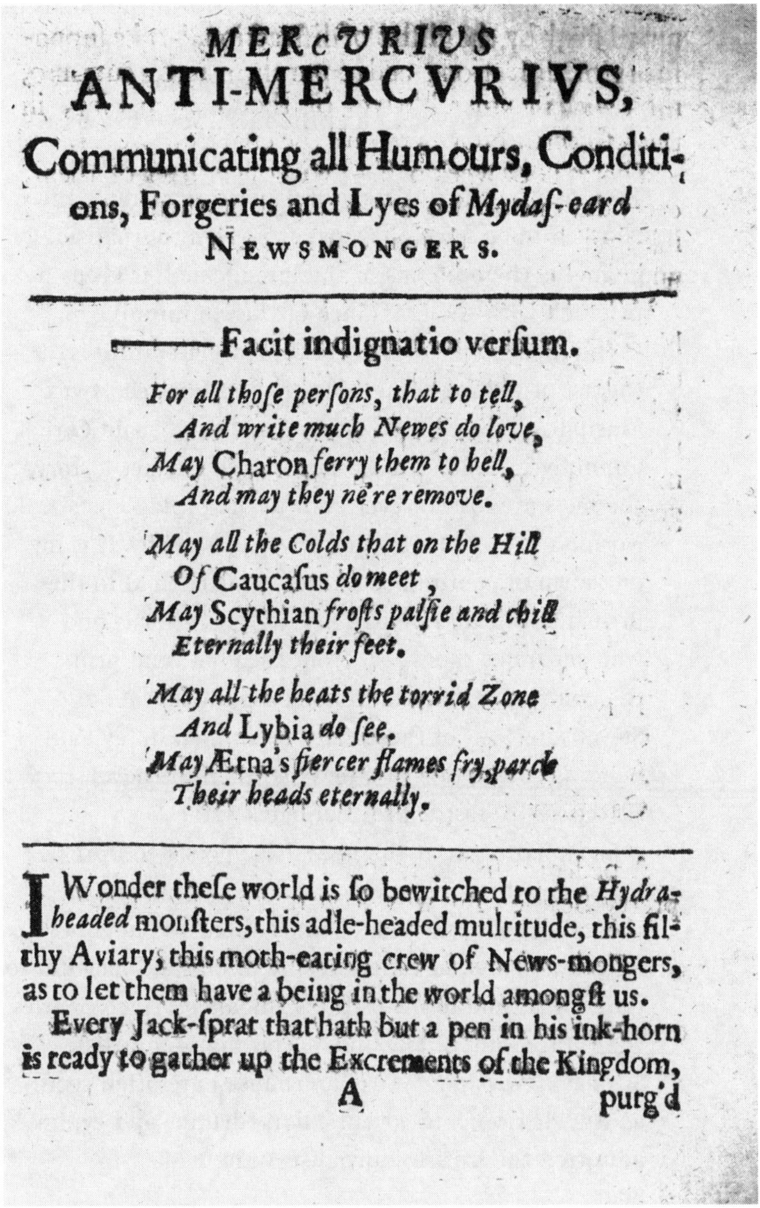

MERCVRIVS
ANTI-MERCVRIVS,
Communicating all Humours, Conditions, Forgeries and Lyes of *Mydaf-eard*
NEWSMONGERS.

———Facit indignatio verſum.

For all thoſe perſons, that to tell,
And write much Newes do love,
May Charon ferry them to hell,
And may they ne're remove.

May all the Colds that on the Hill
Of Caucaſus do meet,
May Scythian froſts palſie and chill
Eternally their feet.

May all the heats the torrid Zone
And Lybia do ſee.
May Ætna's fiercer flames fry, parde
Their heads eternally.

I Wonder theſe world is ſo bewitched to the *Hydra-headed* monſters, this adle-headed multitude, this filthy Aviary, this moth-eating crew of News-mongers, as to let them have a being in the world amongſt us.

Every Jack-ſprat that hath but a pen in his ink-horn is ready to gather up the Excrements of the Kingdom,
A purg'd

Fig. 1.1. Condemnation of newspapers.

newspaper press . . . is to a large extent in the hands of writers who have no respect for propriety or reticence of language',[30] claimed Henry Reeve, in 1889.

'In the old days men had the rack. Now they have the press',[31] the writer and wit Oscar Wilde said in 1891, and another of his vicious witticisms ran: 'There is much to be said in favour of modern journalism. By giving us the opinions of the uneducated, it keeps us in touch with the ignorance of the community.'[32]

The moans and groans continued: 'Literature is the art of writing something that will be read twice; journalism that will be grasped at once',[33] said Cyril Connolly in 1938. 'Once a newspaper touches a story, the facts are lost for ever even to the protagonists', said Norman Mailer. 'I read the newspaper avidly. It is my one form of continuous fiction', is attributed to the British politician Aneurin Bevan. 'An editor is one who separates the wheat from the chaff and prints the chaff', asserted the American politician Adlai Stevenson.[34] All of these can be summed up by Saul Bellow's description of a newspaper in his novel *Herzog*, as 'A hostile broth of black print'.[35]

Complaints about the press have persisted into the twenty-first century: 'Awkward, cantankerous, cynical, bloody minded, at times intrusive, at times inaccurate, and, at times, deeply unfair and harmful to individuals and to institutions', moaned Prince Charles, the future king of England, according to a British Sunday newspaper.[36] 'We [journalists] are often seen as strawberry-nosed voyeurs, liars, drunks and cynics',[37] admitted the British journalist Andrew Marr in 2004.

Yet many of those who grumble about the media are gluttonous gobblers of newspapers and magazines, radio and television. This seems strange: one would not expect something so apparently disliked to be so eagerly swallowed up by readers and viewers. And one wonders how many of these moaners actually read the 'high' literature some of them claim to admire so much.

Two possibilities exist. On the one hand, titillating trivia might be so much junk food for the mind: gulping down gobbets of news could be the mental equivalent of scoffing candy bars, tempting tit-bits which provide instant satiety rather than long-term sustenance. 'High' literature might then be the wholesome, nourishing diet required for long-term mental fitness. On the other hand, given the long-standing nature of the problem, perhaps some deeper reasons exist. This book will consider this puzzle.

Chapters 2–3 will peel away some of the layers of development which underlie newspapers, and show that, like an old tree, they have acquired multiple new skins: old oral traditions have been interwoven with, and partly covered over by, later written conventions.

Chapters 4–7 will continue to examine the evolution of newspapers and other media. Chapters 8 and 9 will look at some of the goals of literature, and assess to what extent they are compatible with the aims of journalism. A final chapter, chapter 10, will discuss the role of journalists, and assess where journalism might be going in the twenty-first century.

CHAPTER TWO

Singers of tales

Oral narrative

The art of narrative song was perfected . . . long before the
advent of writing. It had no need of stylus or brush.

Albert Lord, *The singer of tales* (1960)[1]

Humans have possibly always entertained one
another. Language developed around 70,000 years ago
(chapter 1), yet true writing systems arose only in the
last 10,000 years (as will be outlined in chapter 3). In
those intervening millennia, skilled performers
undoubtedly beguiled their listeners with songs
and stories.

But early oral performances were not purely for
entertainment. More importantly, perhaps, our ancestors orally preserved essential knowledge. Unravelling
some of this from the clouds of time may help us to
understand our own culture. The oral traditions of
previous millennia may be the direct ancestors of
modern journalism. These inherited layers have affected present-day speakers and writers in ways not always
recognized. This chapter will consider these old strands.

Stored wisdom

Modern literature, especially poetry, tends to be thought of as an optional extra, the icing on the cake of culture. But in preliterate societies, oral performances had a more basic role: they contained the stored wisdom of generations.

Passed-down knowledge is often referred to in the Bible: 'Hear, ye children, the instruction of a father. Get wisdom, get understanding: forget it not, neither decline from the words of my mouth';[2] 'Because the preacher was wise, he taught the people knowledge . . . he sought out and set in order many proverbs'.[3]

Such handed down cultural advice is widespread in preliterate societies, including our own Indo-European dynasty. English is one of a largish group of Indian and European languages. Their presumed ancestor, Proto-Indo-European, can be dated back to around 15,000 or even 20,000 BP,[4] and its poetry had a serious purpose. As one writer expressed it:

What we term Indo-European poetry was rather a society's sum of knowledge, which was orally transmitted. The features which our western tradition ascribes to poetry (feeling, inspiration, individualism, participation, etc.) . . . were for Indo-European poetry only a side issue . . . The main thing was to preserve and increase cultural elements which presented something essential to the well-being of the society. We are speaking of the magic spells . . . , the legal formulas . . . , the prayers . . . , the eulogies . . . He who fulfilled such important functions held a position of the first rank in his society.[5]

Exactly where the ancestral language of the Indo-Europeans was first spoken is disputed, though the steppes of Russia is one of a number of possible candidates for the Indo-European 'homeland'. Quite a lot can be gleaned about the Proto-Indo-Europeans from later languages.

Key words enable the cultural background to be sketched out.[6] The Proto-Indo-Europeans worshipped a sky-god: the name of the Greek god *Zeus* comes from the word for 'sky', and Latin *Jupiter* is 'sky-father'. The early Indo-Europeans lived in a patriarchal society: numerous words for a husband's relatives can be reconstructed, but very few for a wife's. A decimal system was in use, shown by the fact that words for 11 to 100 are mostly formed from the numbers 1 to 10. The Proto-Indo-Europeans rode horses and had discovered bronze, since words for these are found in just about all the 'daughter' languages. But more than single words can sometimes be reconstructed.

A number of ancient phrases have been preserved, glued-together chunks that were built into old rituals and poetic narratives. A newish field of study sometimes labelled 'comparative Indo-European poetics' has begun to explore 'proto-poetics', and to make suggestions about these old layers.[7]

Occasionally, the exact words of old phrases are retained. At other times, a literal translation or *calque* – a French word meaning a 'tracing' – is found (as when in the twentieth century the English word *sky-scraper* was 'traced' and emerged in French as *gratte-ciel* 'scrape-sky', or German as *Wolkenkratzer* 'cloud-scratcher').

Some phrases and calques date back thousands of years. The Indo-European languages had a two-part expression denoting wealth, for non-movable and movable possessions. This is found in the Greek epic the *Odyssey*: Odysseus' son Telemachus complains that while Odysseus is away fighting in the war against Troy, would-be suitors of Odysseus' wife Penelope have installed themselves in his palace, and are devouring *keiméliá te próbasín te*,[8] 'riches which lie and riches which move', in other words, the totality of his wealth. This concept, with its components in the same order, dates back well over 2,000 years. It surfaces in English in the legal-sounding phrase *goods and chattels*, originally *good(e)s and cattel(s)*, with the last word being a form of our own word *cattle*.[9]

Another widely used old phrase is one meaning 'imperishable fame', in Greek *kléos áphthiton*.[10] This has an exact early equivalent in Sanskrit, the old Indian language, the precursor of Hindi.

The slaying of a dragon seems to be a stock Indo-European theme.[11] A further recurring image is one of souls flitting from bodies after death: when two major heroes, Patroclus and Hector, are killed on separate occasions in the Greek epic the *Iliad*, the same lines are used to conjure up a pitiful picture of each as a grieving spirit flying to the underworld: 'His spirit flying from his limbs went to Hades, lamenting its fate, leaving behind manhood and youth.'[12] This is not unlike Beowulf's departing soul in the old English narrative poem *Beowulf*, which dates from the first millennium AD: 'From his bosom went his soul to seek the glory of the true.'[13]

Remnants of ancient stylistic conventions are also found, such as a tendency to move the heaviest of several linked words or phrases to the end, as in 'Tom, Dick and Harry', not '!Harry, Dick and Tom', which sounds less natural (an exclamation mark is sometimes used to mark a phrase or sentence that is 'odd' but not ungrammatical). Similarly, we say 'oats, peas, beans and barley grow', 'In the name of the Father, and the Son, and the Holy Ghost'. This has been described as 'X and Y and snaggle-toothed Z',[14] its official name being 'Behagel's law of increasing members'. This 'heaviest last' habit has lingered on in a variety of Indo-European languages.[15] In the *Iliad*, when several names are listed, only the last receives an epithet, as in the 'Catalogue of ships', supposedly a list of the troops serving in the Trojan war:

> Those who . . . lived in Chalcis and Eretria and richly-vined Histiaia.[16]
>
> Those who . . . lived in Pharis and Sparta and Messene with its multiple doves.[17]
>
> Those who lived . . . in Boibe and Glaphura and well-built Iaolkos.[18]

But more interesting, perhaps, than ancient fragments, is how longer sections of narrative were constructed, as will be discussed below.

Song stitching

Greek poetry began with two epics. The *Iliad* describes a section of the famous war between the Greeks and Trojans, and the *Odyssey* recounts the lengthy return of Odysseus from Troy to his home on the island of

Ithaca. These were reputedly written by someone called 'Homer', and they were performed by traditional bards or 'singers of tales'.

The honour accorded to an outstanding singer of tales is a mark of an oral-based society. The description of the revered bard Demodocus in the *Odyssey* is one of the earliest accounts of this type of performance. The hero Odysseus, on his way back from Troy to his home in Ithaca, has been shipwrecked on the shore of Phaeacia. The inhabitants welcome the stranger, and, to entertain him, the king calls for his bard: 'Bring on our god-inspired singer of tales, Demodocus. To him, god has granted the gift of song, to give delight on whatever theme his spirit inspires him to sing.'[19] Demodocus is blind, emphasizing the lack of a written text: 'An attendant went to fetch the god-inspired singer . . . and came back, leading the loyal and trusted bard, whom the muse loved exceptionally. To him, she had bestowed a mixture of good and bad. She had deprived him of his eyes, but had given him a delightful ability to sing and narrate tales.' Bards such as Demodocus had a high status, because of their high skill level. 'Such singers of tales are honoured by all men on earth',[20] Odysseus comments.

Yet Homer's epics are not the polished output of a single genius. They are skilfully crafted patchwork, a bundle of old folk songs, masterfully cobbled together by centuries of talented bards. Old themes have been re-used, and old formulas recombined. The epics inherited from the Greeks, the *Iliad* and the *Odyssey*, are the latest version of centuries of traditional oral epic. The bards were master-craftsmen who 'stitched songs together'. As Walter Ong has expressed it:

> In the *Iliad* and the *Odyssey* Homer was normally taken to be fully accomplished, consummately skilled. Yet it now began to appear that he had some kind of phrase book in his head. Careful study . . . showed that he repeated formula after formula. The meaning of the Greek term 'rhapsodize' *rhapsōid-ein*, 'to stitch songs together' (*rhaptein* 'to stitch'; *ōide* 'song') became ominous; Homer stitched together prefabricated parts. Instead of a creator, you had an assembly line worker.[21]

A humorous poem by Rudyard Kipling highlights the recycling process:

> When 'Omer smote 'is bloomin' lyre,
> He'd 'eard men sing by land an' sea,
> An' what he thought 'e might require,
> 'E went an' took – the same as me!
>
> The market-girls an' fishermen,
> The shepherds an' the sailors too,
> They 'eard old songs turn up again,
> But kep' it quiet – same as you!
>
> They knew 'e stole – 'e knowed they knowed.
> They didn't tell, nor make a fuss,
> But winked at 'Omer down the road,
> An' 'e winked back – the same as us.[22]

This creates a problem for modern readers, since writers and students today are advised not to use clichés, nor to copy others:

> How to live with the fact that the Homeric poems . . . appeared to be made up of clichés? . . . it became evident that only a tiny fraction of the words in the *Iliad* and the

Odyssey were not part of formulas, and to a degree, devastatingly predictable formulas.

Moreover, the standardized formulas were grouped around equally standardized themes, such as the council, the gathering of the army, the despoiling of the vanquished, . . . and so on and on.[23]

Yet what we in modern times might regard as 'plagiarism' is in a preliterate society the normal, skilled re-working of traditional themes and phrases. As Kipling wrote in another poem:

> There are nine and sixty ways of constructing tribal lays,
> And – every – single – one – of – them – is – right![24]

A repertoire of similar themes and formulas is found in oral discourse around the world. This was pointed out in the early twentieth century by Milman Parry, who was possibly the first person to realize that the Greek epics, the *Iliad* and the *Odyssey*, supposedly the works of 'Homer', were traditional oral epic.

The creative methods used to compose the Greek epics showed strong similarities to some relatively recent Balkan examples of oral poetry, which are also highly formulaic in style, Parry pointed out. He defined a formula as 'a group of words which is regularly employed, under the same metrical conditions, to express a given essential idea'.[25] Working in the first third of the twentieth century, Parry was the first to show that formulas functioned as the 'building blocks' of Homeric verse, and that the *Iliad* and the *Odyssey* incorporated a centuries-old oral tradition.

Several strands are involved in the composition process. A basic layer is musical and rhythmic. The

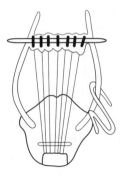

Fig. 2.1. Ancient lyre.

bard accompanied himself on a lyre. In the *Odyssey*, Demodocus is unable to proceed without this instrument, since it has to be fetched for each instalment of his recital. When Alcinous, king of Phaeacia wanted further entertainment, this time in the open air, he commands: 'And someone go and fetch Demodocus his melodious lyre, which was left inside.'[26]

Rhythm and music are useful memory aids: the Homeric epics are written in hexameter metre, comprising six metrical 'feet', with long and short syllables interleaved, usually dum-didi, dum-didi, dum-didi, dum-didi, dum-didi, dum-dum, which give it a 'pacy' feel.

The impression of pace is aided by the simple grammar. 'And . . . and . . . and', runs the story line, with relatively little subordination. Partly prefabricated chunks, stories within stories are woven in, as in the following, which could well have been included in order to please a traveller from Ephyrus: 'There is a city, Ephyrus, in a corner of horse-rearing Argos. Here Sisyphus lived, most splendid of men, Sisyphus son of

Aiolus. He sired a son Glaukus, and Glaukus sired noble Bellerophontes.'[27]

This passage sheds light on another major strand, one of story recollection. Demodocus has numerous stories committed to memory, each ready to be regurgitated in a unique way. Some he selects himself and he sings others in response to requests. In the performances reported in the *Odyssey*, the bard sang on three contrasting topics. His first narrative was a quarrel between two Greek heroes, Odysseus and Achilles. A second was more light-hearted, a story of adultery committed by the god Ares and the goddess Aphrodite. Aphrodite's husband Hephaistos discovered this couple making love, and was furious. As the master-craftsman of the gods, Hephaistos wove a fine mesh over the copulating couple, trapping them so they could not move. Then he invited the other gods to view them. The goddesses out of modesty stayed away, but the male gods had no such qualms, and 'Unquenchable laughter broke out among the blessed gods, when they saw the craft of Hephaistos.'[28] Demodocus' final narrative was one proposed by Odysseus, about the making of the wooden horse, the means by which the Greeks eventually tricked their way inside Troy and captured it, showing that a good singer was able to respond to requests for well-known stories.

Pre-prepared building blocks

But the most important feature is the recreation of the stories afresh each time they are performed. A bard's outstanding memory feat is possible because

ready-made formulas function as 'building blocks'. As
Ong points out: 'In a primary oral culture . . . you have
to do your thinking in mnemonic patterns, shaped for
ready oral recurrence. Your thought must come into
being in heavily rhythmic balanced patterns . . . for
retention and ready recall.'[29] All the major heroes had
a range of personal epithets attached to them, each
one fitting into a portion of a line, usually the beginning or the end. We hear of 'swift-footed Achilles',
'noble Achilles', 'Achilles son of Peleus', 'Odysseus of
many wiles', and so on. 'The deployment of a partly
fixed phraseology is a fundamental aspect of Homer's
style and technique',[30] comments the Homeric scholar
G. S. Kirk.

Some other words also have their own metrical
location: a descriptive adverb *smerdaléon* meaning
'horribly, terribly, terrifyingly' occurs at the beginning
of lines. In one place, it describes the glare of an angry
serpent which has eaten poisonous herbs, thought to
be the source of a snake's venom: 'Like a serpent in its
mountain hole, which has swallowed poisonous herbs,
a fierce anger enters it. *Terrifyingly* it glares, as it twists
and writhes in its hole.'[31] In another place, *smerdaléon*
is used of the bellow uttered by the furious Hephaistos,
when he discovered his wife's unfaithfulness:

> *Terrifyingly* he shouted, calling aloud to all the gods:
> 'Father Zeus, and you other blessed eternal gods,
> come . . .'[32]

This word is more notable for its place in the line
than for its exact meaning. Odysseus himself is described as *smerdaléos* when he emerged from the sea in

Phaeacia after his shipwreck and long immersion in
the water:

> *Terrifying* he appeared with his hair caked in brine.[33]

But sometimes these old phrases, handed down
from generation to generation, became misunderstood.
Such misunderstandings are a sure sign of centuries
of oral tradition.

The 'flower' of youth

The formulaic building blocks were handed down
for generations, as two types of evidence show. First,
lines which do not fit properly into the full hexameter
rhythm reveal sound changes which happened maybe
centuries earlier. Many rhythm-wrecking words originally contained a weak sound (a 'digamma') which
faded out of Greek before classical times.

A second type of evidence of a long oral tradition is
the use of words with shifting meaning. Some of these
have an old, lost sense in some lines, yet a newer, more
recent meaning in others.

Take the word *ánthos*.[34] In classical Greek it meant
'flower', and this meaning can be seen in the English
words *chrysanthemum* 'golden flower', and *anthology* 'a
bouquet of words'. In a few Homeric passages, *ánthos*
has its classical Greek 'flower' meaning, as when bees
fly over spring blooms.[35]

But in early Greek, *ánthos* had a different meaning.
A clue to this is found in Vedic, an early form of Sanskrit, the old Indian language, where *andhas*, a word
related in form to Greek *ánthos*, is something which

horses ate: 'like Indra's horses consuming the *andhas*'.[36]
Here *andhas* was likely to be a type of vegetation,
though probably not flowers.

And in some Homeric passages, the word is
most unlikely to mean 'flower'. Instead, it appears to
mean 'upward shoots', as when a ram is described as
grazing on the 'tender "flowers" of grass'.[37] This ram is
more plausibly grazing on blades or shoots of grass
than on Greek wild flowers. Elsewhere, the word *ánthos*
'upward growth' is contrasted with the word *rízda*
'root': a wild boar is said to drag down trees, with their
roots and their 'flowers'.[38] The Greek phrase is rather
like the English expression 'root and branch'. The
frenzied boar uprooted whole trees, from top to
bottom. In short, *ánthos* meaning 'shoot, upward
growth' was once the opposite of *rízda* 'root,
downward growth'.

That famous poetic phrase 'the flower of youth',
'bloom of youth', found in translations of Homer, may
therefore be a mistranslation. The phrase is superfi-
cially odd, because metaphors are rare in Homer. But if
the word *ánthos* is translated as 'upward growth', the
passage in which it occurs immediately makes sense:
'he had the upward growth of youth',[39] that is, he
was a young man just beginning to sprout whiskers.
And young men killed before any down 'flowered' on
their cheeks[40] are young men killed before their
whiskers or beards had grown.

The phrase 'the upward growth of youth' was
wrongly thought of as a metaphorical phrase 'the
flower of youth'. It was translated into Latin, and
eventually crept into English as a charming cliché,

where it could refer to women as well as men. Tennyson (1830) writes that: 'A simple maiden in her flower / Is worth a thousand coats of arms.'[41] Tennyson might not have found the idea of a whiskery maiden so enchanting, if he had realized the earlier meaning of the phrase!

And so it continues. In the twentieth century, the singer–songwriter Joni Mitchell continued the idea of 'blooming youth':

> Under neon signs
> A girl was in bloom
> And a woman was fading
> In a suburban room.[42]

But the 'flower of youth' example is one only of a number of Homeric layers which can be unravelled. Various other phrases were misunderstood by generations of bards, a firm indication that the epics had developed orally over several centuries. A Homeric phrase *Telamónios Aías* is usually translated as 'Ajax son of Telamon'. Yet Telamon is a shadowy figure, who has no firm genealogy. On closer inspection, the end-of-line epithet formula 'big Telamonian Ajax' occurs in various places, but notably in a battle scene in which Ajax faces 'big plumed-helmet Hector' in a passage of the *Iliad* which is thought to be an archaic layer. Ajax's battle equipment varies in the course of the *Iliad*. But in this oldish passage, it is unusual. He has a long body shield of a type thought to date back to Mycenaean times, 1200 BC or earlier. This body shield is worn slung over his left shoulder by means of a wide strap, a *telamon*. He also has a second *telamon* over his

other shoulder, to secure his sword. It now seems unlikely that Ajax was ever the 'son of Telamon', and the epithet 'Telamonian' probably refers to his equipment, which was of a type so ancient that it did not make sense to the later Greeks, who carried circular shields. Later bards, unfamiliar with this archaic battle-gear, reinterpreted the word 'Telamonian' to mean the 'son of Telamon'.[43]

The epics attributed to 'Homer' are now realized to be the work of multiple folk-bards: 'The entire language of the Homeric poems . . . was best explained . . . as a language generated over the years by epic poets using old set expressions which they preserved and/or reworked largely for metrical purposes.'[44] Eventually, they were written down, probably around 650 BC in the recently developed Greek alphabet. Clearly, a master-craftsman was in charge of the final pulling together of the various versions of the *Iliad* and the *Odyssey*, and an authorized text was settled in Athens in the sixth century BC.

Yet for generations, oral epic conventions seeped into the literature of the Greeks, and even into our own. As Walter Ong comments:

Oral formulaic thought and expression ride deep in consciousness and the unconscious, and they do not vanish as soon as one used to them takes pen in hand . . . Early written poetry everywhere . . . is at first necessarily a mimicking in script of oral performance . . . You scratch out on a surface words you imagine yourself saying aloud in some realizable oral setting. Only very gradually does writing become composition in writing . . . that is put together without a feeling that the one writing is actually speaking aloud.[45]

British bards

Even our own culture has been affected by an old oral tradition, though the evidence is not always easy to find.

In the eighteenth century, rumours abounded that an ancient bardic tradition still existed in Scotland. Lured by these reports, Samuel Johnson and James Boswell travelled to the Western Isles of Scotland, hoping to gather evidence of these old strands. Johnson explains:

It seems to be universally supposed that much of the local history was preserved by the Bards, of whom one is said to have been retained by every great family . . . They said that a great family had a Bard and a Senachi, who were the poet and historian of the house . . . but that neither Bard nor Senachi had existed for some centuries.[46]

Johnson was disappointed not to find these, but comforted himself with the belief that as they could neither read nor write, their knowledge was of little value, and their utterances primitive: 'The Bard was a barbarian among barbarians, who, knowing nothing himself, lived with others who knew no more.'[47] And, he (wrongly) claimed: 'There may possibly be books without a polished language, but there can be no polished language without books.'[48]

Yet in spite of Johnson's pessimism, due in part to his false belief that an illiterate nation must be a primitive and barbarous one, the British Isles still contains signs of an earlier flourishing oral tradition. The most obvious legacy may be the folk beliefs enshrined in 'sage saws':

The North wind shall blow,
And we shall have snow.

Early to bed and early to rise,
Makes a child healthy, wealthy and wise.

Red sky at night, shepherd's delight
Red sky in the morning, sailor's warning.

As with all oral knowledge, the words of these old maxims vary: the red sky couplet sometimes refers to shepherds, sometimes to sailors.

But more important oral strands exist, though these have largely been ignored by standard 'literature'. Until relatively recently, English writers were presumed to be a highly educated minority, for whom writing was essential: 'Diction, merely vocal, is always in its childhood',[49] Johnson pompously, and wrongly, asserted. The English and Scottish descendants of Indo-European 'singers of tales' were virtually ignored. Yet we have an inherited repertoire of old folk-ballads, which were once found throughout Great Britain, though they are now tucked away in printed pages and rarely sung, or sung only by a minority. But our old ballads are clearly part of the Indo-European bardic tradition: 'Traditionally and primarily, a ballad is an oral narrative poem, often sung to a simple instrumental accompaniment. Such works may have passed through several generations and been adapted by many presenters.'[50]

Most ballads are complete narratives, and are like the mini-stories which are sometimes found within the *Iliad* and *Odyssey*. Many ballads also have parallels in German folk-lore. A massive collection of the English

and Scottish ballads was made in the nineteenth
century by Francis James Child.[51] He found regret-
tably few live oral ballads, according to G. L. Kittredge,
who wrote the preface to Child's massive collection:
'Mr Child made an effort to stimulate the collection
of such remains of the traditional ballad as still live
on the lips of the people . . . The harvest was, in his
opinion, rather scanty; . . . Enough was done at all
events, to make it clear that little of value remained to
be collected in this way.'[52] But the written versions are
by no means insignificant, and typically run to several
variants for each ballad. They preserve enough for us to
see that these narrative, metrical poems fit in with
what we know of traditional oral song, with recurring
epithets, such as *milk-white steed*, *lily-white hand*, repetition of verses with minor alterations, and simple syntax. The need for poetic rhythm has also been handed
down, though in a slightly altered form. Indo-European
metre, including Greek epic, was originally based on
quantity, the alternation of long and short syllables.
In English, this has changed to a system of heavy
(strong) versus light (weak) syllables.

The basic story of a ballad often comes across clearly,
though the main participants may be given different
names in the different variants. One ballad, versions of
which are found in both England and Europe, is known
as 'Lady Isabel and the Elf-Knight'.[53] A young woman, a
'maiden', sometimes referred to as a king's daughter, is
wooed by an 'outlandish' (a non-local) knight. After he
has demanded a substantial dowry, they both ride
away on horseback, the horses being part of the
dowry:

> She mounted on her milk-white steed
> He on the dapple grey;
> They rode till they came unto the sea-side,
> Three hours before it was day.

At this point, the knight showed that he was a
scheming and practised multiple-murderer:

> Light-off, light off thy milk-white steed,
> And deliver it unto me;
> Six pretty maids I have drownded here,
> And thou the seventh shall be.

He then commanded her to undress:

> Pull off, pull off, thy silken gown
> And deliver it unto me;
> Methinks it looks too rich and too gay,
> To rot in the salt sea.

In the next two verses, he tells her to pull off her
silken stays, and finally, the last layer, her Holland
smock. She objects, asking him to turn his back,
saying that she does not want such a ruffian to
see her naked. Then:

> He turned his back toward her,
> And viewed the leaves so green;
> She catched him round the middle so small,
> And tumbled him into the stream.

He begs her to take hold of his hand, and pull him out,
to which she replies:

> Lie there, lie there, you false-hearted man,
> Lie there instead of me.
> Six pretty maids have you drowned here,
> And the seventh has drowned thee.

At this, 'She mounted on her milk-white steed,
And led the dappled grey', and went home. But this is
not the end of the story. Her pet parrot appears to have
knowledge of the drowning, and she promises to give
it a cage made of glittering gold, with a door of
ivory, to ensure its silence.

The various versions all have the same basic
plot, though the name of the heroine changes: Lady
Isabel, an unnamed king's daughter, May Colven, May
Colin. The villain also alters: he is an elf-knight, a
bloody knight, false Sir John. In one version, a harp
is even mentioned, played by the knight, suggesting
that bards standardly accompanied themselves with
musical instruments:

> He's taen a harp into his hand
> He's harped them all asleep.[54]

But Child's collection of ballads is not our only
source of knowledge. We can piece together more
about the old ballad tradition than we might realize,
by looking at the history of newspapers, where street
ballads were the forerunners of popular tabloids.
These were, however, fundamentally altered in
nature by the fact that they were written.

This chapter has looked at oral narrative,
which preceded written language by tens of thousands
of years. The next chapter will explore the invention
of writing, and discuss the relationship between
spoken speech and written language.

CHAPTER THREE

The tongue of the hand

Speech and writing

The pen is the tongue of the hand – a silent utterer of words
for the eye.

> Henry Ward Beecher, *Proverbs from Plymouth Pulpit* (1887)[1]

In its earliest stages, language was almost certainly
spoken, not signed or written. Spoken language has two
powerful advantages: it can be used in the dark, and
it frees the hands for other uses.

In the eighteenth century, signing was (wrongly)
assumed to be primitive and universal: 'The universal
language that your scholars have sought for in vain . . .
is here; it is right before your eyes, it is the mimicry
of the impoverished deaf . . . it alone will provide
you with the key to all languages', exulted the
eighteenth-century writer Abbé de l'Epée.[2]

But sign languages turn out to be fairly different
from one another around the world, and not universal
at all[3] despite the fact that occasional gestures, such as
pointing, recur. Sign languages in humans emerge
spontaneously only when the main spoken route is

unavailable, though a mature sign language is a complete language system, which can express everything found in spoken or written language.[4]

Some animals have been taught a simplified version of sign language, the most famous being the chimp Washoe. But Washoe cannot be said to have language, in the sense that human signers have language.[5]

For humans, writing is more widespread than sign, though compared with spoken language it was a late starter, arriving tens of thousands of years later. Spoken language emerged over 50,000 years ago (chapter 2), and writing is not more than about 10,000 years old. 'The two oldest and greatest inventions of man were the wheel and the art of controlling fire . . . if one wished to make a group of three, surely the development of writing must claim the third place', it has been suggested.[6] This chapter will discuss its invention, and will look at how it interacts with spoken language.

Proto-writing and counting

Nobody is quite sure when writing first emerged. The historian is faced with an array of visual signs, often called 'proto-writing', used for information storage and communication. They include decorations on objects such as pottery vessels, message sticks, clay pebbles, knotted cords, and seal impressions marking property, among others.[7]

The first problem is how to distinguish proto-writing from writing proper. The second is to understand how true writing arose.

At one time, the origin of writing was thought
to be simple: 'At the basis of all writing stands the
picture',[8] argued Ignace Gelb, a Professor at the University of Chicago, in a widely praised book called *A study
of writing* (1963). Pictures then became schematized, he
assumed: 'That the geometric designs are schematic
developments from picture forms can be proved con-
clusively from the observation of the development of
any writing in its historical stages',[9] he asserted.

But this view now turns out to be wrong. Counting,
not pictures, may be the key to early writing. Humans
have possibly always counted: 'For *Fingers*, by ordinance
of nature, and the unrepeatable statute of the great
Arithmetician, were appointed to serve for casting
counters, as quicke and native digits, alwaies ready at
Hand to assist us in our computation', claimed
John Bulwer in 1644.[10]

And some modern researchers agree. Ildefonso,
a deaf Mexican who was without language until he
was an adult, acquired numbers more readily than
signs for words. This supports those who argue for the
naturalness of numerosity. His teacher described his
progress: 'Slowly, I wrote 1 through 20 and placed the
corresponding crayons above each numeral. Ildefonso
studied what I had written, and got it without any
more help. He found the symbols for numbers easy
compared to signs for words. Apparently arithmetic
already resided in his brain.'[11] As the neuropsycho-
logist Brian Butterworth expresses it: 'Everyone
counts . . . we are born with special circuitry in our
brains for categorising the world in terms of
numerosities . . . The use of numbers is so universal

that it is reasonable to infer that everyone is born with a Number Module. I shall call this the Mathematical Brain hypothesis.'[12]

Our earliest record of numbers may be an inscribed bone, known as the Lartet Bone. Found in the Dordogne, France, it dates from around 30,000 BP, and has a series of markings which are neither random, nor decorative. The marks are grouped, and the groups organized into larger patterns. Arguably, they represent the phases of the moon.[13] These marks seem to show that humans were counting at this time, and that they knew how to make written marks expressing numerosity.

The markings on the Lartet Bone are controversial. But other evidence points to a prehistoric use of numbers. In the late 1960s, a French woman, Denise Schmandt-Besserat, based then at Harvard, began a research project investigating when and how clay came to be used in western Asia.[14] She looked at clay artefacts which dated back to between 8,000 and 11,000 years ago, an era which saw the firm establishment of the first farming settlements in this area. Alongside the beads, bricks and figurines she had expected, she also found 'an unforeseen category of objects: small clay artefacts of various forms',[15] which had been fired to ensure durability. They might be some kind of token, she suspected, though they had often been overlooked or misclassified in museum collections: 'When the tokens were noted, the heading might read "objects of uncertain purpose," "children's playthings," "game-pieces" or "amulets"'.[16] One archaeologist identified them as amulets, suggesting that they

Fig. 3.1. Early clay tokens.

expressed a desire for 'personal identification', and another commented on five mysterious clay objects 'looking like nothing in the world but suppositories. What they were used for is anyone's guess.'[17]

But Schmandt-Besserat was more realistic: 'It cannot simply be coincidence that the first tokens appear early in the Neolithic period, a time of profound change in human society. It was then that an earlier subsistence pattern, based on hunting and gathering, was transformed by . . . the development of a farming way of life',[18] she pointed out. Food storage might have required these early farmers to record which part of the annual crop yield should be allocated for the farm family's own subsistence, what should be set aside for seed for next year's crop, and what part used for barter. 'It seems possible that the need to keep track of such allocations and transactions was enough to stimulate development of a recording system', she proposed.[19]

In Mesopotamia, writing proper when it eventually emerged around 5,000 BP may not have been the result of pure invention. Instead, it was a novel application of this counting and recording system that had been in existence for thousands of years, Schmandt-Besserat suggested. And a close relationship between counting and embryonic writing has been observed elsewhere: in Central America, an elaborate calendrical system was at the heart of early Mayan writing.[20]

In short, the development of a number system may have been a crucial early phase in the emergence of writing: humans first used written marks to record important numerical information. Then mature writing developed. Mesopotamian writing was not the source of all writing systems in the world, as was once assumed: Chinese and Mayan writing almost certainly developed independently. The once popular monogenesis (single origin) of writing theory has now been abandoned.

But several crucial stages intervened between the first emergence of mature writing, and the development of our own alphabet.

The alphabet

Early writing was something of a mish-mash, with a mixture of ideograms – symbols which express whole concepts (modern examples are = 'equals', 6 'six') – and logograms – symbols which represent linguistic units

tiripode   aikeu   keresijo   weke   2

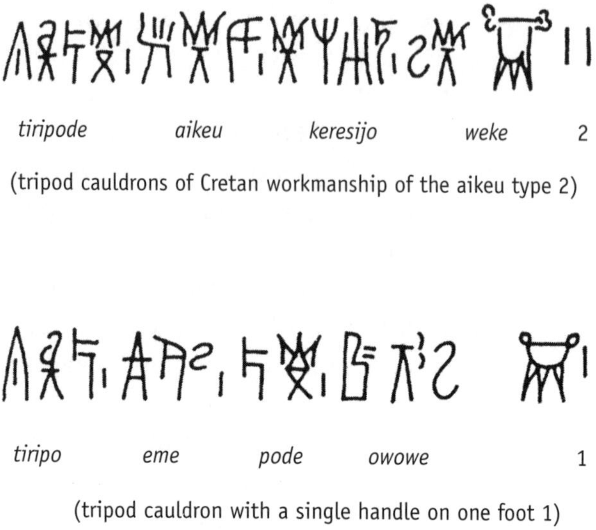

(tripod cauldrons of Cretan workmanship of the aikeu type 2)

tiripo   eme   pode   owowe   1

(tripod cauldron with a single handle on one foot 1)

Fig. 3.2. 'Tripod' tablet (section).

such as syllables or phonemes. In the Greek dialect Mycenaean, for example, a famous tablet dating from halfway through the second millennium BC showed a picture of a tripod, followed by signs for the syllables *ti-ri-po-de*, and the numeral 2.[21]

Logograms are signs which have lost any explicit pictorial meaning, and become signs for sounds, though often imperfect ones. In the Mycenaean example above, the Greek word *tripodes* 'tripods' had its first consonant cluster unwrapped from *tri* to *ti-ri*, and the *-s* was left off the end of the word.

Our alphabet came about by means of the so-called 'rebus principle', with a *rebus* defined as 'a representation of words or syllables by pictures of objects or by symbols whose names resemble the intended words or syllables in sound'.[22] To take a modern example, a picture of the sun could stand for either 'sun' or (rebus) 'son', or a picture of an eye could stand for either 'eye' or (rebus) 'I'. Rebuses have come into fashion recently in text-messaging, with 2 standing for 'to' or 'too' as well as 'two', and 4 standing for 'for' as well as 'four', as in *t2g* 'time to go', *t4t* 'time for tea'.[23]

Our alphabet is 'a Roman adaptation of a Greek adaptation of a Semitic adaptation of an Egyptian adaptation of signs first used beside the Euphrates river in the city of Sumer, later called Babylon, four thousand years before Christ', as one writer expressed it.[24] In terms of writing systems, the rebuses started out as Egyptian hieroglyphs, which were adapted to form an early Semitic alphabet, which was developed by the Phoenicians, then further adapted by the Greeks and Romans.[25] For example, an Egyptian hieroglyph with a wavy line meant 'water'. This became the Semitic *mem*, the forerunner of Greek *mu*, now our letter *m*. An Egyptian hieroglyph representing a folding door was taken over as the Semitic *daleth*, which became Greek *delta*, now transformed into our letter *d*.

'The alphabet is the most flexible and useful method of writing ever invented . . . and has become the nearly universal basis for the scripts employed by civilised peoples', it has been claimed.[26] Yet our alphabet was flawed from the beginning. The Semitic system from which it was derived did not show vowels, so the Greeks who adopted it had to adapt some symbols for this purpose. The Latin-speaking Romans took over the alphabet from the Greeks, and spread it around their empire. Our own alphabet is essentially the Roman one, though English has more vowels than Latin, and also several different sounds, such as [θ] in *thin* and [ð] in *then*. No wonder the correspondence between English speech and writing is problematic!

English speech–writing disharmony

'My spelling is Wobbly. It's good spelling but it Wobbles, and the letters get in the wrong places', said the bear Pooh, in A. A. Milne's children's book *Winnie the Pooh*.[27] Pooh was explaining why he was unable to write 'Happy birthday' on the birthday present he was planning to give his friend Owl. Pooh is not alone in being unhappy about spelling. Pip in Charles Dickens's novel *Great Expectations* 'struggled through the alphabet as if it had been a bramble-bush, getting considerably worried and scratched by every letter'.[28] 'Written forms obscure our view of language, they are not so much a garment as a disguise', Saussure famously said.[29] Richard Chenevix Trench complained in the nineteenth century:

The intention of the written word . . . is by aid of symbols agreed on before, to represent to the eye with the greatest accuracy which is possible the spoken word.

It never fulfils this intention completely, and by degrees more and more imperfectly. Short as man's spoken word often falls of his thought, his written word falls often as short of his spoken. Several causes contribute to this.[30]

The would-be spelling reformer Alexander Ellis pointed out in 1845 that the word 'orthography' could

just as well be written *eolotthowghrhoighuay*, by analogy
with G*e*orge, c*o*l*o*nel, Ma*tt*hew, kn*o*wledge, *gh*ost,
*rh*eumatic, Beauv*oir*, lau*gh* and qu*ay*. In the early
twentieth century, the playwright Bernard Shaw
reputedly suggested that *ghoti* could spell 'fish',
with *gh* as in 'rough', *o* as in 'women' and *ti* as in
'station'.[31]

Comic poets have long exploited the confusion
which could arise when the same sound can be
represented by different letters, and the same letter
may stand for a variety of sounds:

> Owe, beam my bride, my deer, rye prey,
>   And here mice size beef ore rye dye;
> Oak caste mean knot tin scorn neigh way –
>   Yew are the apple love me nigh![32]

'O be my bride, my dear, I pray, and hear my sighs
before I die; O cast me not in scorn away – you are the
apple of mine eye!'

More recently, the use of spell-checkers in word-
processing programs has resulted in a plethora of such
amusing oddities. The problem is that many letter
sequences form words which would be accepted by the
program's spell-checker:

> Eye have a spelling chequer;
> it came with my pea sea.
> It plain lee marques four my revue
> miss steaks eye canne not sea. . .
> Four eye have run this pome threw it;
> And I'm shore you're pleased two no –
> It's letter perfick awl the weigh;
> my chequer tolled me sew.[33]

'I have a spelling checker, it came with my PC. It plainly marks for my review mistakes I cannot see. . . . For I have run this poem through it; And I'm sure you're pleased to know – It's letter perfect all the way; my checker told me so.'

Against spelling reform

Every so often, some enthusiast pleads for English spelling to be revised: 'Our spelling must be reformed . . . Now, economics, humanity and our position in the world demand a switch to rational spelling. One can only hope that action is taken before it is too late', begged an article in the *Oxford Magazine* in 2002.[34]

Yet spelling reform is unlikely to happen, at least in the near future. It would have as many disadvantages as advantages. Our spelling holds together widely flung varieties of English: Californians, Londoners and Indians would find it hard to communicate in writing if our spelling was changed.

Spelling also sometimes enables links between words to be revealed, connections that are partially hidden by the pronunciation, as in *society - social, division - divisive, right - righteous, allege - allegation, please – pleasant*.

These points have been obvious for a long time. They were pointed out by Jonathan Swift in the early eighteenth century. He speaks of:

A foolish opinion advanced of late years that we ought to spell exactly as we speak: which besides the obvious inconvenience of utterly destroying our etymology, would be a thing we should never see an end of. Not only the several

towns and counties of England have different ways of pro-
nouncing, but even here in London they chop their words
after one manner about the court, another in the city, and
a third in the suburbs; and in a few years, it is probable,
will all differ from themselves, as fancy or fashion shall
direct; all which reduced to writing would entirely
confound orthography.[35]

A further advantage of our 'wonky' spelling is
that we can instantly distinguish between differently
spelled homonyms (words with different meanings
which sound the same), as in 'She asked for a pear/
pair', 'Where's the kernel/colonel?', 'Taxes/taxis can be
a problem', and so on. This can be very useful, and
avoids the confusion that sometimes arises in spoken
speech, as when a customer phoned a technical support help-line for advice on a computer problem:

> TS (Technical support): I need you to right-click on the
> open desktop.
> C (Customer): Okay.
> TS: Did you get a pop-up menu?
> C: No.
> TS: Okay. Right-click again. Do you see a pop-up menu?
> C: No.
> TS: Can you tell me what you have done up until now?
> C: You said write 'click', so I wrote 'click'.[36]

Yet our spelling system is not quite as wonky as is
sometimes claimed. The impression that it is chaotic
is an illusion. Over 80 per cent of words are spelled
regularly, and only 3 per cent are so unpredictable that
they have to be learned as a special case, according
to a computer analysis carried out in America.[37] The
superficial impression of bizarre irregularity is due to
the fact that many of the words which are spelled

unpredictably are high-frequency everyday words, such as *the, one, though, through, head,* and so on.

And if spelling reform did take place, the whole of past literature would be unavailable to those who knew only the new system. It would be prohibitively expensive to convert whole libraries, so anyone who wanted to browse through oldish books and newspapers would have to learn the old system in any case. Spelling reform is therefore not a viable option, at least for the time being – though email and text messaging might be the forerunners of an eventual partial reform. *wd u b wilin 2 hlp me?* 'Would you be willing to help me?' ran a recent email message sent to me. And the following poem won a text poetry competition organized by a national newspaper:

PIC ME UP
I left my pictur on the ground wher u walk
so that somday if th sun was jst right
& th rain didn't wash me awa u might c me
out of th corner of yr I & pic me up.
Emma Passmore[38]

As this poem shows, it is important not to change too much, or understanding would be affected. The poem has *c* 'see', *i* 'eye', *u* 'you', but otherwise mainly leaves the final letter off words – *awa(y), pic(k), pictur(e), th(e), wher(e)* – though occasionally one in the middle: *j(u)st, som(e)day.* Some text messaging is already inconsistent with differently pronounced words such as *cud* 'could', *cum* 'come', spelled with the same middle letter.[39]

Maybe minor alterations will creep permanently into the language via text messaging. As the journalist

Jeremy Clarkson noted, commenting on his daughter's language: 'What she may not grow out of . . . is her insistence that "today" is spelt with a 2 and that "great" somehow has an 8 in it. This new language has now spilt from the mobile phone into her thank-you letters and homework' (Fig. 4.3, p. 46).[40]

Equal but different

'Language and writing are two distinct systems of signs; the second exists for the sole purpose of representing the first', according to Saussure.[41] This is something of an exaggeration, though it is broadly true that 'all systems of writing are demonstrably based upon units of spoken language'.[42]

Saussure's emphasis on speech was a much-needed attempt to counterbalance a widespread view among the educated that written forms should be valued more highly than spoken: 'The literary language adds to the undeserved importance of writing',[43] he noted. A widespread overemphasis on writing has only recently begun to fade.

In the modern world, 'Equal but different' is now generally thought to be the case. This is not at all a new idea. As the nineteenth-century writer Richard Chenevix Trench pointed out:

Every word . . . has *two* existences, as a spoken word and a written; and you have no right to sacrifice one of these, or to subordinate it wholly, to the other. A word exists as truly for the eye as for the ear; and in a highly advanced state of society, where reading is almost as universal as speaking, quite as much for the one as for the other.[44]

```
bbl (be back later)
bbs (be back soon)
bfn (bye for now)
brb (be right back)
btw (by the way)
cul8r (see you later)
gr8 (great)
imho (in my humble opinion)
imo (in my opinion)
lol (laughing out loud/lots of love)
np (no problem)
o2l (out to lunch)
oic (oh i see)
rotfl (rolling on the floor laughing)
tb (text back)
tbh (to be honest)
thx, tnx, tx (thanks)
tmb (text me back)
ttfn (ta ta for now)
ty (thank you)
wb (write back)
weg (wicked evil grin)
x! (typical woman!)
y! (typical man!)
yw (you're welcome)
```

Fig. 3.3. Txting (text messaging).

Some differences between speech and writing
are obvious. Speech tends to be inexplicit, written language explicit. Speech tends to be repetitive, written
language often avoids direct repeats. Speech mostly
has a simple structure, and written language is more

complex. A typical example of simple, repetitive, spontaneous spoken speech is illustrated in the following transcription of a woman recounting the time she fainted on the New York subway:

> and I remember saying to myself: 'There is a person over there that's falling to the ground. And that person was me. And I couldn't put together the fact that there was someone fainting and that someone was me. And it was funny because in my head I said . . . my awareness was such . . . that I said to myself 'Gee well, there's a person over there, falling down.' And that person was me.[45]

This informal, repetitive text contrasts strongly with a paragraph from an academic text, which is composed of a single sentence almost seventy words long:

> Earlier theories of genes as static blueprints for body plans have given way to a radically different picture, in which genes move around, recombine with other genes at different points in development, give rise to products which bind directly to other genes (and so regulate their expression) and may even promote beneficial mutation (such that the rate of mutation may be increased under stressful conditions where change is desirable).[46]

This paragraph is reasonably clear. It is not gob-bledygook. But it has been constructed quite differently from the description of the subway fainting episode, and for a different purpose.

These two examples are fairly extreme. On closer examination, many examples of spoken and written language overlap in style, as the Frenchman Jacques Derrida somewhat pompously pointed out: 'Representation mingles with what it represents, to the point where one speaks as one writes, one thinks as if the represented were nothing more than the shadow or reflection of the representer. A dangerous promiscuity and a nefarious complicity between the reflection and the reflected which lets itself be seduced narcissistically.'[47] Detailed statistics now available show how written and spoken styles overlap: novels are sometimes like spoken speech; drama and political speeches are usually scripted; newspaper reportage, emails and a variety of television programmes hover in the middle between spoken and written language.[48]

Puzzlingly, for those who like neat divisions, some clinical conditions, and especially a bizarre affliction known as deep dyslexia, indicate a close link between speech and writing, and show how difficult it can be to separate them. Ordinary (surface) dyslexia is an inability to read, due to optical or neurological problems.[49] But a patient with deep dyslexia looks at a word and pronounces a quite different one, though one that is closely related in meaning. A patient might read *play*, instead of 'drama', *ill* instead of 'sick', *football* instead of 'soccer'.[50] At some deep level, the patient has understood the word he or she is reading, then been unable to retrieve the phonological shape needed to utter it. Neurologists argue about this phenomenon,[51] whose interest lies partly in the light it sheds on the way in which speech and writing may overlap and interweave.

Yet the most important point which arises out of this chapter is the huge discrepancy in date between the origin of language, and the invention of writing. Speech evolved at least 50,000 years before writing was invented. Yet humans have probably always entertained one another with words. Much of our literature and journalism ultimately arose out of oral performances (chapter 2), whose influence is indelibly stamped on much of what we read today, as will be discussed in the following chapters.

CHAPTER FOUR

Hangings, histories, marvels, mysteries

The birth of journalism

> Ballad-mongers on a Market-day
> Taking their stand, one (with as harsh a noyce
> As ever Cart-wheele made) squeakes the sad choice
> Of Tom the Miller with a golden thumbe,
> Who crost in love, ran mad, and deaf and dumbe,
> Halfe part he chants, and will not sing it out,
> But thus bespeakes to his attentive rout:
> Thus much for love I warbled from my brest,
> And gentle friends, for mony take the rest.
>
> William Brown, *Britannia's pastorals* (1616)[1]

A hotchpotch of ear-catching tales of hangings, horrors, histories, alongside marvels, murders, monsters and mysteries, were sold to the public by ballad-mongers, from the late fifteenth century onward. The songs of the traditional minstrels had been converted by the invention of printing (1476) into a trade in broadsides, or broadsheets, single sheets which were printed on one side of the page only. (The name *broadsheet* is these days attached to our 'serious'

newspapers, and is not to be confused with the
earlier use of the term.)

'The broadside ballad was an adaptation of the
older traditional minstrelsy to the newer demands of
topicality, a kind of music journalism, and the forerunner of the popular press',[2] points out Leslie Shepherd,
one of the first people to work seriously on this topic.
These broadsheets combined both news and entertainment, and are the direct predecessors of today's so-called
'tabloids'. (Our word *tabloid* is a printing term, which
refers to a newspaper of compact size. It came to be
associated with popular, lurid newspapers, though
is now becoming outdated as our current serious
newspapers are increasingly printed in a compact
format.)

Penny dreadfuls

The sellers of (old-style) broadsheets were in it
for the money. They were salesmen, not skilled
performers. They might sing sections of their star
stories in order to entice customers, but often did so
very badly, like the ballad-monger described at the
top of this chapter. The object was to advertise their
wares, not to provide artistic entertainment. The
printed sheet they were trying to flog to their
customers was more important to them than
the commercial promoting it.

By 1641, the standard cost of a broadsheet was a
penny: 'For a peny you may have all the Newes in
England, of Murders, Flouds, Witches, Fires, Tempests

Fig. 4.1. Ballad singer.

and what not', in one of Martin Parkers 'Ballads', Martin Parker being 'the most famous and popular ballad writer of the seventeenth century'.[3]

The broadsheets were found in alehouses and markets, and were partly targeted at the working classes, as in Shakespeare's play *The winter's tale* (1610), where the roguish Autolycus peddles ballads to gullible purchasers:

CLOWN: What hast thou here? Ballads?

MOPSA (a shepherdess): Pray now, buy some: I love a ballad in print, a-life, for then we are sure they are true.

AUTOLYCUS: Here's one to a very doleful tune, how a userer's wife was brought to bed of twenty money-bags at a burden; and how she longed to eat adders' heads and toads carbonadoed.

MOPSA: Is it true, think you?

AUTOLYCUS: Very true, and but a month old . . . Here's another ballad of a fish that appeared upon the coast on Wednesday the fourscore of April, forty thousand fathom above water, and sung this ballad against the hard heart of maids: it was thought that this was a woman and was turned into a cold fish for she would not exchange flesh with one that loved her. The ballad is very pitiful and as true.[4]

But some noblemen and gentry were also enthusiastic purchasers. The seventeenth-century London diarist Samuel Pepys was known to have a collection. The broadsheets took their material from a variety of sources, some news (often much exaggerated), old scandals, hideous crimes, traditional ballads, weird monsters – anything which would appeal to the popular imagination, the 'attentive rout'.

The broadsheets were printed in clumsy Gothic type, known as 'blackletter', with woodcut illustrations. Relatively few (about 250) still survive, and not all of them are singable. One called 'The true description of this marveilous straunge fish' (1569) contains a prose account of a bizarre fish caught between Dover and Calais, and shows a picture of this marine marvel, with ten fins, and a tail looping round like that of a cat.[5]

Execution broadsheets were in high demand. One early example was headed: 'A proper newe Ballad,

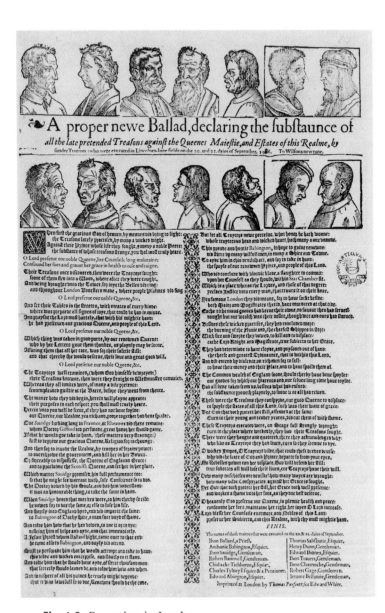

Fig. 4.2. Execution in London.

declaring the substaunce of all the late pretended
Treasons against the Queenes Maiestie, and Estates
of this Realme, by sundry Traytors, who were executed
in Lincolnes-Inne fields on the 20, and 21, daies of
September, 1586' (Fig. 4.3).[6]

The criminals had plotted to assassinate
Elizabeth 1, and planned to crown Mary, Queen
of Scots, in her place. The broadsheet's heading was
surrounded by rough head-and-shoulders drawings of
fourteen men, the supposed traitors, whose names
were listed at the bottom. A note was added that
the verses were to be sung 'To Wilsons new tune'.
Twenty-four blackletter verses described the plot,
containing lines such as:

> This proud and hautie Babbington, in hope to gain renowne
> did stirre up many wilful men, in many a Shire and Towne.
> To aid him in this devilish act, and for to take in hand:
> the spoyle of our renowned prince, and people of this Land.

Certain topics were perennially popular. The
heroic outlaw Robin Hood remained a core source of
interest. Dozens of extant ballads celebrate his exploits:
'Of all the sources from which the fertile muse of the
English ballad-maker has derived its subjects, no one
has proved more inexhaustible, or more universally
acceptable to the hearers, than the life and adventures
of Robin Hood', commented William Chappell, in
'Popular Music of the Olden Time', in 1859.[7] Robin
Hood is thought to have been based on a genuine
historical figure, whose death has been dated to the
mid thirteenth century, though the stories which

are attached to his name may have come from several sources.

Around 40 Robin Hood verse narratives are printed in Francis James Child's mammoth compilation of folk ballads (mentioned in chapter 2). The longest contains almost 2,000 lines, consisting of 456 4-line stanzas.[8] It begins:

> Lythe and listin, gentilmen,
>   That be of frebore blode;
> I shall tel you of a gode yeman,
>   His name was Robyn Hode.

Some of the Robin Hood ballads contain traditional phrases, such as 'lily-white hand', as in the following account of the trickery which led to Robin's death.[9] Robin was ill, and the usual medical treatment in those days was blood-letting. Robin was bled to death by a treacherous prioress, supposedly a trusted cousin:

> She took him by the lily-white hand,
> And led him to a private room,
> And there she blooded bold Robin Hood,
> While one drop of blood would run down.

> She blooded him in a vein of the arm,
> And locked him up in the room
> Then he did bleed all the live-long day,
> Until the next day at noon...

Robin is too weak to escape, but calls out of the window to his trusty companion, Little John:

> Lay me a green sod under my head,
> And another at my feet;
> And lay my bent bow by my side,
> Which was my music sweet;

And make my grave of gravel and green,
Which is most right and meet.

Most of the verses in this ballad contain four lines.
This six-liner appears to contain two specially inserted
for the occasion, about Robin's bow. They may be an
adaptation from an earlier ballad in which the main
character asked to be brought a musical instrument, since 'music sweet' is mentioned. And so
Robin died:

Thus he that never feard bow nor spear
Was murdered by letting blood;
And so, loving friends, the story it ends
Of valiant Robin Hood.

As the evergreen Robin Hood theme shows, a
mythologized past was popular. Fact and fiction were
intertwined in a sometimes inextricable mix, as in
'The Death of Queen Jane', which gives an account
of the childbirth and subsequent death of Jane
Seymour, wife of Henry VIII:

Queen Jane was in labour full six weeks or more,
And the women were weary, and fain would give o'er:
'O women, O women, as women ye be,
Rip open my two sides, and save my baby!'

'O royal Queen Jane, that thing may not be;
We'll send for King Henry to come unto thee.'
King Henry came to her, and sate on her bed;
'What ails my dear lady, her eyes look so red?'

'O royal King Henry, do one thing for me:
Rip open my two sides, and save my baby!'
'O royal Queen Jane, that thing will not do:
If I lose your fair body, I'll lose your baby too.'

She wept and she waild, and she wrung her hands sore;
O the flour of England must flurish no more!

> She wept and she waild till she fell in a swound,
> They opend her two sides, and the baby was found.
>
> The baby was christened with joy and much mirth,
> While poor Queen Jane's body lay cold under earth.[10]

In the version quoted above, Jane was supposedly in labour for six weeks, though other versions have (more plausibly) three days. In another variant, Jane was given a 'cordial' to dull the pain, and only one side was opened, not two as in the version quoted earlier:

> Then they gave her some cordial which put her in a swound,
> And her right side was opened and her baby was found.[11]

The 'flour' or 'flower' of England is mentioned in more than one account, as when King Henry is at first unwilling for his wife to be operated on:

> 'Oh no', says King Henry, 'that's a thing I'll never do.
> If I lose the flower of England I shall lose the branch too.'[12]

This is reminiscent of the 'flower of youth' found in Greek epic (chapter 2).

But in spite of these dramatic descriptions of Jane Seymour's supposed Caesarian delivery and death, she probably gave birth to her son Edward in the normal way on 12 October 1537, 'but, in consequence of imprudent management, died twelve days after',[13] possibly of puerperal fever.

Quite a lot is known about broadside ballads, because from the mid sixteenth century (1557) printers were required by law to register them with the Stationers' Company. Around 1,500 were registered before 1600.[14] Allowing for gaps in the Stationers' Register, and also for the fact that not everybody registered them as they should, roughly 3,000 distinct ballads were published in the second half of the sixteenth century, it has been estimated.[15]

Publishers and booksellers treated them as a sideline. In the year 1520, the Oxford bookseller John Dorne, for example, sold 170 ballads for a halfpenny each, with concessions for buying in quantity: 7 for threepence or 12 for fivepence.[16]

George Puttenham, a key sixteenth-century literary figure, described them somewhat scornfully in *The art of poesie* (1589).[17] According to him, they were performed by street performers, and 'blind harpers or such like tavern minstrels that give a fit of mirth for a groat, and their matters being for the most part stories of old time . . . [and song] made purposely for recreation of the common people at Christmasse diners and brideales, and in tavernes and alehouses, and other places of base resort'.

A long tradition of complaint about the popular press probably began around this time. Tudor rulers were concerned about the effect of ballads on their subjects. Henry VIII banned offensive ballads in 1533 and 1542, and similar proclamations were made in the reigns of Edward VI and Mary.[18]

Broadsheets were limited in size, and, as literacy increased, demand arose for something lengthier than a single sheet of paper. The result was a plethora of chapbooks.

Popular pamphlets

Chapbooks were small, popular pamphlets, sold by itinerant dealers known as chapmen. From around

1500, they gradually replaced the single-page broadsheets. They first grew up alongside them, with overlapping subject matter, then supplanted them. Chapbooks contained between four and twenty-four pages, and were quite tiny by today's standards, about five and a half by three and a half inches (15 × 10 cm), smaller than a modern-day paperback.

Between around 1550 and 1700, these little pamphlets proliferated: forty-two publishers between 1560 and 1622 produced chapbooks, according to one estimate,[19] and they outsold books, we hear in 1592: 'Chapmen, able to spread more pamphlets . . . than all the booksellers in London'.[20]

The staple fare of the old broadsheets was continued in chapbooks, with miracles, monsters, witchcraft, unusual weather and sensational murders in abundance. But the chapbooks covered a wider range of topics. They were forerunners perhaps of modern magazines – or weekend supplements.

Different publishers had their own specialities. One chapbook on popular medicine (1630) was called *The kings medicines for the plague*, supposedly issued by 'the whole colledge of physitians'.[21] Another was called *The poore-mans plaster box* (1634),[22] and was a practical guide to first-aid, written for 'the poore and plaine people, such as cannot . . . get a Chirurgion, or else . . . want meanes to pay them'. Serious bruises may be caused when 'men in building fall from off the house'. Then 'if the man faln or bruised be so poore that he hath no bed to sweat in', one should 'set him for to sweat in horse dung up to the chin'. Another, by the same publisher, was a courtship handbook: *Cupids schoole:*

wherein, yongmen and maide may learne divers sorts of complements (1632).

Other publishers dealt with sermons and religious works, such as *The life and death of the virgin Mary* (1620).[23] General moral diatribes are also found. *A looking glasse for drunkards* (1627) by 'George Shawe minister of Gods word' condemned drunkenness: 'For as wet and foggy ground in the summer time doe ingender multitudes of frogs and toads, and other venomous vermine: So doth drunkeness produce and ingender multitudes of diseases in the body of man.'[24]

In this type of output, England seems to have been behind the European mainland, where so called 'canards', on crime, miracles, floods and heavenly apparitions were published earlier, and some translations came to England.[25]

But just as broadside ballads overlapped with chapbooks, so chapbooks overlapped with newsbooks. Broadsheets and chapbooks were media appetizers only, compared with the newsbooks and newspapers which followed.

Newsbooks

Newsbooks, dating from the mid seventeenth century, are often regarded as the first 'true' newspapers, in that they consistently contained accounts of current events. They also continued the tradition of combining information and entertainment.

English newsbooks were late in getting established, compared with those on the European mainland, partly because it was at one time illegal to print domestic news in England. Nevertheless, some unlicensed printing went on from around 1620. Nobody is quite sure how much, but some accounts suggest that dozens of illegal rags may have been around: 'The liberty of these times, wherein your courants, gazettes, pasquils, and the like, swarm too abundantly. (1626).'[26] Ben Jonson in his play *The staple of news* (1631) pours scorn on these unreliable publications: 'the age . . . hunger and thirst after published pamphlets of news, set out every Saturday but made all at home, and no syllable of truth in them; than which there cannot be a greater disease in nature, or a fouler scorn put upon the times'.[27]

The proliferating undercover publications had various names. *Currants, courants, corantos* were from the French *courir* 'run', and originally meant 'express message'. *Gazette* comes from the Italian *gazetta*, possibly the small Venetian coin with which such a rag was purchased (compare our own phrase 'penny-dreadful'). *Pasquil* comes from a Latin word meaning a posted-up lampoon. Other names found were *diurnal*, originally the same word as *journal*, meaning a record of daily occurrences. Another was *mercury* from Mercury, the speedy messenger of the gods. Finally, *newsbook* took over as the most popular term. This was 'a small newspaper. In common use from around 1650 to 1700', according to the *Oxford English Dictionary*.

The word *news*

The word *news* is only a little more than 400 years old . . . Of the several English synonyms, *tydings* seems to be the oldest.

But the thing itself is almost as old as the hills. The child of
chance and curiosity and simple wonder, it must have had its
origin in the earliest awakenings of human intelligence.[28]

This pompous comment was made in the first half of
the twentieth century, and it sums up 'news' then and
now. It always has been, and still is, a well-stirred broth
combining information and entertainment.

The word *news* was originally plural, as is obvious
from its form. 'He was right pensyve and sore troubled
with those newes', wrote Lord John Bourchier Berners
in 1523.[29] 'Euil newes neuer come too late' runs a pro-
verb from 1574.[30] Proverbs often preserve archaic linguistic usages, and even before this time *news* was
increasingly found in the singular: 'I hearde speak
of it, when ye newes therof was brought to Pope Iulie
the seconde' is dated 1566 in the *Oxford English
Dictionary*.[31]

The word *news* is singular in Shakespeare's plays.
In Richard III, which was written about 1593, Richard
greets Stanley with 'Stanley, what news with you?'[32]
to which Stanley replies: 'None good my liege'. And
Cymbal, a character in Ben Jonson's play *The staple
of news*, also uses a singular form in his comment:
'When Newes is printed, it leaues Sir to be Newes.'[33]

As with many new usages, the word took time to
get established. At one time, *news*, spelled sometimes
nuses, could also mean 'items of news': 'At that time
there came two important nuses' (1641).[34] *To news* was
also found as a verb, meaning 'to report': 'This being
newsed about the Town, many afterwards shunned
the occasion of meeting with the Prince' ran a
report in 1650.[35]

In the eighteenth century, the word *news* came
also to have the meaning of 'newspaper'. 'You know
his House was burnt down to the Ground, Yes; it was
in the News' runs a quotation from Jonathan Swift in
1738,[36] and this usage is also found in an entry in
Samuel Johnson's famous dictionary (1755), the second
meaning of *news* being 'Papers which give an account
of the transactions of the present times'.[37]

The first 'real' newsbook

The rise of newsbooks is particularly connected
with the civil war which broke out in England in 1642.
Both the royalists, who supported the king, and the
parliamentarians, who opposed him, published
accounts of the proceedings.

The first newsbook proper appeared on the streets
of London, probably around Holborn and Farringdon,
on 29 November 1641, and was called 'The Heads of
Severall Proceedings in this Present Parliament'.[38] It
covered news from Ireland, the debate over 'The
Grand Remonstrance' (which was a history of King
Charles's wrongs), and the banishing to the Tower of
a certain Master Palmer. It is written in order of
occurrence, and Palmer's banishment comes in the
last sentence: 'Thursday, morning they againe fell
into debate about Master Palmer, and it was put to
the question and agreed upon that he should be
sent to the Tower.'

Several newsbooks were on sale, though two of these
civil war newsbooks were the most famous: *Mercurius
Aulicus*, published by the royalists and produced in

Numb. 44

A PERFECT DIVRNALL OF THE PASSAGES In Parliament :

From the 10. *of Aprill to the* 17· *of Aprill.*

Collected by the same hand that formerly drew up the Copy for William Cook
of Furnifulls Inne , *and now printed by* J. Okes, Fr. Leach, *and are
to be sold by* Fr. Coles *in the Old Baily.* 1643·

Munday the 10. *of Aprill.*

THe House of Commons received information
that divers persons through the neglect of
the Courts of Guard come daily to London
from Oxford, and other parts of the Kings
Army, notwithstanding their former order
against it; and they thereupon drew up an
other order to this effect. That whatsoever
person shall come from Oxford, or any part
of the Kings Army to London, or any parts
adjacent, or to any other part of the Army
under the Command of the Earle of Essex,
or to any Fort, or Court of Guard, kept by
the authority of both Houses of Parliament,
or of the Lord Generall the Earle of Essex,
shall apprehend as Spies and Intelligencers,
and be proceeded against according to the Rules and grounds of War; and it is
X 2   further

Two messages
from his Ma-
jesty, and the
Parliaments
answer, the L:
Generals his
advance, Sir
Will. Wallers
happy successe
& other mat-
ters of note
this weeke.

Fig. 4.3. A PERFECT DIURNALL OF THE PASSAGES In Parliament,
10 April 1643.

Oxford, and *Mercurius Britannicus*, the parliamentary newsbook. Print runs were around 500, but people passed them from one to another, so many more than 500 readers perused each issue.

The newsbooks were published irregularly, usually every few days. They contained primarily accounts of events in the war, but also included some shock-horror stories.

The narrative keeps strictly to order of occurrence. In the following account,[39] a modern newspaper would probably have created a headline 'SAVED BY HIS HAIR', and moved the dramatic hair story to the first paragraph, rather than the last. By modern standards, the early part of the story is dull in the extreme:

Also, there was letters read from Sir Iohn Hotham, informing that the Cavaleers have made divers attempts by night against Hull, tending to burne the same in severall places, and that whilst the Souldiers should be busie in quenching the fire, they would scale the Walls and seize upon the Town; but this enterprise was prevented by Sir Iohn Hothams vigilancy, who so played upon them with his Cannon shot, that they soone left the enterprize, only they burned two Wind-Mills, which belonged to Hull.

But the last section is riveting, even to a modern reader:

The Earle of Newport . . . was by the waft of a Cannon shot dismounted from his horse, and cast into a deep ditch of water, where had he not been catcht hold of by the haire of the head, after once or twice sinking, he had lost his life: which passage being afterwards told to his Majesty, the Archbishop of York being present, made answer it was well his Lordship was not a Roundhead, if hee had, he might have been drowned, for that then he would have had little haire on his head to have been holden by.

Similarly, the lengthy and pedestrian description of the events leading up to the execution of Captain Hotham is tedious.[40] The following is a short extract only:

Captaine Hotham . . . was about eleven of the Clock this forenoone brought from the Tower, to the place of Execution on Tower-Hill. At his first coming upon the Scaffold Mr. Coleman Minister of the Tower, and an other Minister, had some conference with him, admonishing him to cleere his conscience both towards God and man, after which Mr. Coleman made an excellent Prayer for the occasion, Captaine Hotham joyning with him, and after that the Captaine made prayer himself, and at the ending thereof stood up, and turned to the people, made a short Speech . . .

A modern newspaper would possibly have begun with the execution itself, or even the touching final section, in which the severed head is wrapped up by the victim's brother: 'Upon the conclusion of his speech, Mr. Coleman prayed againe, at the ending whereof Captaine Hotham prepared himselfe for the Block, whereon having laid his head, the Executioner severed the same from his body at one blow, which his Brother Master Durant Hotham standing by tooke up, wrapt in a Scarfe, and laid it in the Coffen.'

A number of the reports are especially tedious to read, such as the account of the following troop movements:

On Sonday, April 22 Colonel Ingoldsby having notice of Col. Lamberts being with a party near Daventry, marched with his own Regiment, Captain Linleys Troop of Col. Rossiter's

Regiment, and two Companies of Col. Streaters Regiment,
commanded by the Colonel himself to the place where
Lambert was, about two miles distant from Daventry, with
four Troops of Horse, viz. Col Alureds and Major
Nelthrops . . . Captain Hesilrigg's Troop and Captain Clare's
Troop, besides several Anabaptists, Quakers, and Other
Fanaticks. Col Ingoldsby's Folorn commanded by Cap.
Elsemore, met with Cap Hesilrigg, whom he took prisoner.[41]

A propaganda war takes place alongside the
battles and troop movements. The following anecdote
of bestiality is probably an attempt by the royalists to
discredit their parliamentarian opponents, at the
same time providing titillation for readers:

on Sunday last Decemb.9 while His Majesties Forces were
at Church, one of their Prisoners was missed by his Keeper,
who searching for him, and looking through a cranny into
the Stable, he saw a ladder erected, and the holy Rebell . . .
committing Buggery on the Keepers owne Mare. The Keeper
seizing on him, brought him instantly before Sir Roger
Leveson, where being examined, he openly and plainly
confessed the whole fact, for which they will speedily
proceed against him, though the poore Keeper is like to
loose his Mare which (according to the Statute) must be
burned to death.[42]

Some of these anecdotes may be primarily for
entertainment, but even these sometimes include a
'crime and punishment' moral, as in the following
account, where a man's bad behaviour is followed by a
permanent deterioration in his health: 'at Norwich, . . .
a bold bad man did pull down his breeches at the
Communion Table, and laide there his most odious
and nasty burden, but observe and tremble at the
divine vengeance, he was suddenly tormented with

the griping in his guts, and lamentable roaring out, he was never able to go to the stool afterwards'.[43]

Some of the stories seem unbelievably bloodthirsty to modern readers, and are also shocking in relation to the treatment of women, as in the following story of the revenge of a jealous wife:

Many strange disasters have fallen out this week, viz. at Cobham in Kent, a woman jealous of her husband, sent for the suspected female, and having drunk freely with her, she at the last demanded of her, if she would have her nose cut off, or her bearing part; and immediatly she and her maid servant fell to work, and exercised that part of her body which they thought had most offended. Not long after her husband came home, and demanding what there was to eat, she replyed, that she had got the best bit which he loved in the world, and so presented him with that most ungrateful object. Amazed at the horrour of it, he addressed himself to the constable, who carrying both Mistriss and Maid to the next Justice, they were both committeed to Maidstone Goal; But the dismembered woman being not dead, they put in great bayl to be answerable to justice.[44]

Another blood-thirsty shock-horror story, which also contains a 'crime will be punished' message, is found in the following report of the execution of a child murderer:

There has been a remarkable piece of Justice done at Mastricht of late worth taking notice of; A woman having lamentably murthered her husbands child he had by a former wife, was afterwards apprehended; who presently confessed the fact and was thereupon sentenced to be executed after the same manner. In the River of the Mase where she had flung in her child, was a scaffold built, upon which she was brought, and strangled at a stake, and presently her hands and legs were chopt off with the same chopping knife wherewith she had cut off those of her childe, and afterwards she was put into a bag and flung into the Mase.[45]

Yet such horrific stories are less usual than those in which some freak of nature is described, such as the 'child with two tongues': 'In the Suburbs of London, in the lower end of East Smithfield, at a place called Knockfergus, a young woman was brought to bed with a Child that was born with two Tongues, the one in some measure covering the other, but the lower Tongue appearing to be the more firm and longer than the other.'[46]

Those who complain that newspaper standards have lowered in recent years should maybe compare some modern stories with those found in old newsbooks.

Complaints about newsbooks

Cheap newsbooks were 'Calculated exactly to the low and sordid Capacities of the Vulgar', and were the subject of numerous complaints. Some of these were mentioned in chapter 1, more are listed below:

Newsbooks were cheap, and looked cheap, being 'weekly Fragments' and mere 'penny-worths of History', 'peny-worths of paper', 'penniworths of impiety'. Their news was either invented or so utterly distorted that they were 'so many impostumated Fancies, so many Bladders of their own Blowing', full of 'parboyl'd Non-sense'. Accordingly the authors were 'a company of impudent snakes', a 'Generation of Vipers' . . . They 'gull'd' their readers 'out of their money' . . . Greed . . . [and] falsehood both led

the perfidious newsbook writer to aim at the uneducated,
'poore deluded People', the 'credulous Vulgar'
'unconsidering persons'.[47]

A clergyman and church historian claimed that 'such
scurrilous papers do more than conceivable mischief',
another called them 'squealing scribes'.

'The tirades against newsbooks formed a tradition
from which subsequent writers continued to draw',[48]
Raymond notes. Hostility to newspapers sometimes
found today is at least as much due to this inherited
tradition of complaint as it is to intelligent reading
of the papers themselves.

The general anxiety about the press in the
seventeenth century led to severe restrictions. In 1649,
for example, a printing act regulating the press was
passed in parliament. In 1666 parliament prohibited
publication of its proceedings.

Yet attempts to muffle the press did not silence
it, and the next century saw the bursting forth of
newspapers as we know them. This will be the
topic of the next chapter.

CHAPTER FIVE

Calendars of roguery and woe

Daily newspapers

Ay – read the newspapers! . . . Daily calendars of roguery and woe! Here, advertisements from quacks, money-lenders, cheap warehouses, and spotted boys with two heads! . . . Turn to the other column – police reports, bankruptcies, swindling, forgery, and a biographical sketch of the snub-nosed man who murdered three little cherubs at Pentonville . . . Turn to the leading article! and your hair will stand on end.

Edward Bulwer-Lytton, Money (1840)[1]

Newspapers are somewhat like mega-stores with multiple departments, compared with the old newsbooks, which were more like specialized high-street shops. The newsbooks contained dull, factual accounts occasionally interleaved with nuggets of titillating scandal (chapter 4). In contrast, newspapers encompass a fairground of variety. The quotation at the top of the chapter from a mid-nineteenth-century play gives some idea of the expanding newspaper content, and the worry this sometimes caused.

In 1702, the first daily newspaper, the *Daily Courant* began publication. Prior to that, newsbooks had appeared only intermittently, every few days, whenever something newsworthy happened, or there was enough material to fill an issue.

Regular newspaper output should be a cause for praise, one would have thought, in that it encouraged literacy. Yet throughout most of the eighteenth century, the press was viewed with suspicion, particularly by politicians. In 1712, a tax was levied on newspapers, and this was later increased, several times. The publication of parliamentary debates was prohibited. Any accounts which circulated were likely to be gossip handed down in coffee houses, suggested Oliver Goldsmith in 1762: 'from the oracle of some coffee-house, which oracle has himself gathered them the night before from a beau at a gaming-table, who has pillaged his knowledge from a great man's porter, who had his information from the great man's gentleman, who has invented the whole story for his own amusement'.[2]

Towards the end of the century, such restrictions began to be lifted. In 1771, the House of Commons opened up its proceedings to the press, and in 1775 so did the House of Lords. Newspapers proliferated, both morning and evening ones. As George Crabbe wrote in 1785:

> For, soon as morning dawns with roseate hue,
> The 'Herald' of the morn arises too,
> 'Post' after 'Post' succeeds, and all day long
> 'Gazetters' and 'Ledgers' swarm, a motley throng.
> When evening comes she comes with all her train,
> Of 'Ledgers', 'Chronicles' and 'Posts' again.[3]

Into the general medley came some of the newspapers which have survived up till the present

day. This chapter will outline their birth and rise or
decline. Today's newspapers are usually divided into
broadsheets (serious newspapers with a high number
of words) on the one hand, and tabloids (with a greater
emphasis on photos and entertainment) on the other.
The name *broadsheets* has been taken over from the old
single-sided broadsides (as noted in chapter 4), though
fairly inappropriately as today's broadsheets contain
multiple pages. Increasingly also, the name *broadsheet*
in its newer sense is a misnomer, as most of the
serious newspapers are now available in compact
(tabloid) format.

Big Daddy

The 'Big Daddy' of them all began in 1785. *The Times*
was originally named the *Daily Universal Register*. It
brought the number of London morning papers to
nine, and was followed soon after by the *Observer* in
1791.

The Times was notable in two main ways. First, it
invested in technology, which enabled its print-run to
outnumber that of other newspapers. Second, it spent
money on getting news fast.

At the beginning of the nineteenth century, 'It
took many hours to strike off the 3000 or 4000 copies,
of which the daily issue of the Times then consisted',
noted James Grant, an early chronicler of newspaper
development.[4] But this was to change.

In 1804 a *Times* compositor, Thomas Martyn,
'produced a model of a self-acting machine for
working the press' but the pressmen were 'so bitterly

hostile to any such innovation, that Martyn was almost placed in fear of his life'. Because John Walter, the proprietor, 'did not at that time possess a very large capital, the scheme fell to the ground'. But 'John Walter bided . . . his time', and in 1814 he decided to try out a steam press patented by Koenig 'in adjoining premises for fear of the hostility of the pressmen'. Koenig and his assistant worked secretly and quietly for 'many months', gradually perfecting the machine: 'The night on which this curious machine was first brought into use in its new abode . . . was one of anxiety and even alarm. The suspicious pressmen had threatened destruction to any one whose inventions might suspend their employment.' The pressmen were told to wait for news from Europe. Then, around six o'clock in the morning, Walter went into the press-room, and told them that *The Times* had already been printed by steam. He was prepared to suppress violence, he said, but if they remained 'peaceable', their wages would be guaranteed until they found similar employment: 'Thus was this most hazardous enterprise undertaken, and successfully carried through; and printing by steam on an almost gigantic scale given to the world.'[5]

Circulation figures leapt. Some writers have assumed that demand for *The Times* increased. But demand was always there, though at first it could not be satisfied. In 1815, fewer than 5,000 copies a day were sold. By 1834, this had risen to 10,000, and by 1844 to more than 20,000. By 1851, the figure had doubled to 40,000, and by 1864, to over 50,000.[6]

Allied to these advances in printing capacity went a preparedness to spend money on getting news fast: 'In

1834 the Times . . . established a system of expresses literally regardless of expense . . . in virtue of which intelligence could be received . . . with the greatest practical expedition'.[7]

Lord Durham had been invited to a great public dinner in Glasgow, and there was 'intense interest to learn what his utterances would be'. *The Times* sent two of its best parliamentary reporters to Glasgow, and positioned relays of postmen and horses at intervals between Glasgow and London. The 400-mile journey was therefore completed at the rate of 15 miles an hour, and the speech appeared in *The Times* a day before it was expected: 'The unprecedented achievement created a great sensation throughout the country.'

The Times also spent money liberally on foreign intelligence, and 'was everywhere spoken of in terms of the warmest commendation'.

The paper had a sober appearance, and a clear but pompous style, as shown by a best-selling issue on the death of Nelson (6 November 1805; see Fig. 5.1):

GLORIOUS AND DECISIVE VICTORY OVER THE COMBINED FLEET, AND DEATH OF LORD NELSON
We know not whether we should mourn or rejoice. The country has gained the most splendid and decisive Victory that has ever graced the naval annals of England; but it has been dearly purchased. *The great and gallant* NELSON *is no more*: he was killed by almost the last shot that was fired by the enemy.

Yet this major announcement was not on the front page, but was inside the newspaper, with no picture attached. A picture finally appeared a few

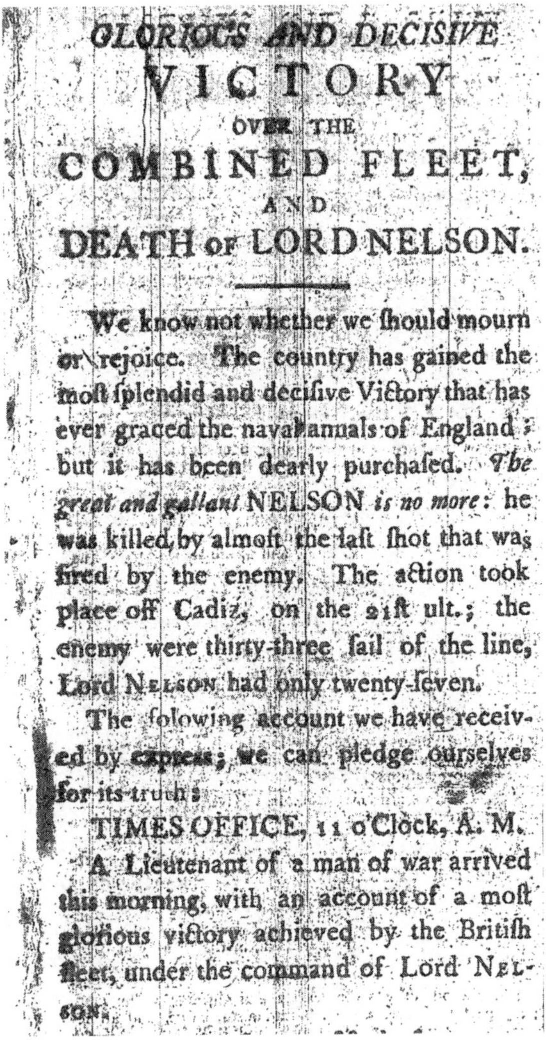

Fig. 5.1. Report of Nelson's death, *The Times*, 6 November 1805.

The enemy's fleet confifted of THIRTY-
THREE fail of the line, with frigates, &c.
They came out of Cadiz on the 19th of
October, and two days afterwards were en-
countered by the Britifh fleet, confifting of
only TWENTY-SEVEN fail of the line,
(feveral having been detached under Rear-
Admiral Louis) with fome fmaller fhips.
The battle continued during four hours,
and ended in the capture of NINETEEN of
the enemy's ships of the line, befides one
which blew up in the action.

The *Victory* being clofely engaged with
feveral of the Enemy's Ships, a Mufket-
fhot wounded Lord NELSON in the Shoulder, and thus terminated a Life of Glory.

A number of Prizes drifted on a lee-
shore, in a gale of wind, a day or two afterwards, and probably many have been
wrecked. Admiral COLLINGWOOD had
ordered that every ship which could not be
brought away, fhould be destroyed. Two,
however, effected their escape into Cadiz.

Admiral VILLENEUVE is a prisoner.
On our side two Captains, we believe
DUFF and COOKE, and three or four
hundred men were killed. We have not
lost a single ship.

Fig. 5.1. (*Cont.*)

days later (10 November 1805) of the funeral car and casket of his ashes, again on an inside page (Fig. 5.2, pp. 80–1).

In the 1830s, a leader writer, Captain Sterling, came to be known as 'The Thunderer' due to his claim that on a political issue: 'We thundered forth the other day an article on the subject of . . .': 'Sentence after sentence in Captain Sterling's leaders rolled forth with a moral majesty which might well be compared to the pealing of thunder in the natural world.'[8] Later, the name 'the Thunderer' became attached to *The Times* itself.

In the 1840s, a huge step forward came in the invention of the 'electric telegraph', which abolished the need for relays of galloping horses and transformed the speed with which messages could be transmitted around the world.

The Times made full use of this new technology. It could by now print over 10,000 copies an hour, and during the Crimean war (1853–6), the sales were occasionally over 70,000 for a single issue. But that was not the record: on the death of Prince Albert in December 1861, the sales-figure was 91,000.

In the first six months of 1855, *The Times* sold over 9 million copies, according to the stamp returns. In comparison, the *Morning Advertizer* and the *Daily News* each sold around a million copies, and the *Morning Chronicle*, the *Morning Post* and the *Morning Herald* around half a million.

The Times was also praised for its size, though this varied. 'So great a quantity of matter' was published on 22 May 'last' (probably 1870) that 'it would require a whole day to read it all',[9] though the record was held

FUNERAL OF LORD NELSON.

Yesterday the burial of this illustrious warrior took place in St. Paul's Cathedral. At an hour before day-light, the drums of the different Volunteer Corps in every part of the Metropolis beat to arms. The summons was quickly obeyed; and, soon after, these troops lined the streets, in two ranks, from St. Paul's Church-yard to the Admiralty. The Life Guards, too, were mounted at their post in Hyde-park at day-break, where the carriages of the Nobility, &c. with the mourning coaches appointed to form part of the Procession, began to assemble. A quarter before six, the bells of St. James's began, at eight o'clock, in a slow rolling sound.

By ten, about one hundred and six carriages were assembled, of which number near sixty were mourning coaches, principally filled with Naval Officers, all of which, under the direction of the proper Officers, were marshalled in their due order of precedence, and proceeded into St. James's Park, to be in readiness to fall into the Procession, on the proper signal.

In St. James's Park were drawn up all the regiments of Cavalry and Infantry, quartered within one hundred miles of London, who had served in the glorious campaigns in Egypt, after the ever-memorable Victory at the Nile; and a detachment of flying artillery, with twelve field pieces, and their ammunition tumbrils. At half past ten, the Procession commenced from the Admiralty, with the march of the several regiments, led by his Royal Highness the Duke of York, attended by his *Aides-du-Camp* and Staff, in the following order :—

A detachment of the 10th Light Dragoons.

Four Companies of the old Highlanders, drums muffled.

The band of the Old Buffs playing solemn dirges, muffled.

The 92d Regiment, in buttons, their colours honourably shattered in the service, covered with crape, which word was inscribed upon them, borne in the centre, and hung with crape.

The remaining Companies of the Old, preceded by their ancient pipes, playing the dead march in Saul.

The 31st and 3d Regiments, with their bands playing as before.

Remainder of the 10th Light Dragoons, trumpets sounding, at intervals, a solemn dirge.

Eleventh Dragoons.

Scots Greys, preceded by Trumpeters sounding the Dead march by Handel.

Detachment of Flying Artillery, with twelve field pieces and tumbrils.

Six Marshalmen, on foot, to clear the way.

Messenger of the College of Arms, in a mourning coach, with a badge of the College on his left shoulder, his staff tipped with silver, and furled with sassnet.

Six Conductors, in mourning cloaks, with black staves headed with Viscounts coronets.

Forty-eight Pensioners from Greenwich Hospital, two and two, in mourning cloaks, with badges of the deceased on their shoulders, and black staves in their hands.

Twelve Marines, and Forty-eight Seamen of his Majesty's ship the Victory, two and two, in their ordinary dress, with black scarfs and stockings, and crape in their hats. Watercoats of the deceased, in black coats, with their badges.

Drum Major.

Trumpeters.

Serjeant Trumpet.

ROUGE CROIX Pursuivant of Arms (alone in a mourning coach), in a close mourning, with his tabard over his cloak, holding his staff.

The STANDARD borne in front of a mourning coach, in which was a Captain of the Royal Navy, supported by two Lieutenants in the front. This Standard, and the other banners, in the succeeding part of the Procession, were composed of damask, having the ornaments emblazoned on them with gold, silver, and colours; and the arms, crests, badges, and devices of the deceased were painted on them. The supporters were Captains in the Royal Navy, in full uniform, black scarfs, breeches, and black stockings, and crape round their arms and hats.

---

partly covered with black velvet. The corners and sides were decorated with black ostrich feathers; the whole festooned with black velvet, richly fringed, immediately above which, in the front, was inscribed, in gold, the word NILE, at one end; on one side, the following motto—" *Hoste devicto, requiescit*:" behind, the word TRAFALGAR: and, on the other side, the motto—" *Palmam qui meruit ferat*," as in the engraving. The carriage was drawn by six led horses, in elegant furniture.

We here present our readers with a representation of the Funeral Car which conveyed the Body of our Great Naval Hero, and of the Coffin, in which his honoured remains are now inclosed.

The only difference in the appearance of the Funeral Car from the engraving is, that it was so far intended, neither the pall, nor coronet, appeared on the coffin. The shot was thrown into the stem of the Car, in order to give the public a complete view of the coffin and the coronet was to make the alteration.

The whole moved on in solemn pace, through the Strand to Temple Bar-gate, where the Lord Mayor of London, with the Corporation, waited to receive the procession. On the arrival of the military procession, the whole, his Lordship advanced, and spoke a few words to his Royal Highness the Duke of York, in which, we presume, he intimated permission for their entrance. As the Procession advanced within the city, the carriages of the Common Council, as had been previously adjusted, fell in before the Physicians of the deceased; the Aldermen and Sheriffs before the Masters in Chancery; and the Prince of Wales and the Heralds at Arms.

Upon the arrival of the Procession at St. Paul's Cathedral, the cavalry marched off to their barracks: the Scotch regiment drew up in the area fronting the Church, and marched into the Western gate, and so remained. The forty-eight Greenwich Pensioners, with forty-eight Seamen and twelve Marines, from the Victory, entered the Western-gate, ascended the steps, and divided in a line on each side under the great Western portico, at the entrance of the Procession entered the Church, dividing on each side, and taking the rank and stations assigned them.

His Royal Highness the Duke of York and his Staff, with the Colonels of Volunteers, followed the Funeral Car on horseback.

On the arrival of the Body and the Funeral Car at the great entrance, it was drawn up without the Western Gate. The Body was taken from the Car, covered with the Pall, and borne by twelve Seamen from the Victory, and was received within the precincts of the Cathedral by the Supporters and the Pall-bearers, who had previously alighted for its reception.

The Cathedral of St. Paul's was filled at an early hour, by all those who could obtain places. From the great length of the procession, and the necessity of attending to the marshalling of the various gradations of ranks, which had been, in some degree, a little overlooked at the York Herald's, length, standing the attention of the York Herald's, length thedral, before the Rouge Croix entered the Cathedral, before the succeeding part of the procession appeared. When, however, it did make its appearance, its effect was uncommonly impressive.

Then followed,

GARTER Principal King of Arms (in a mourning coach), habited by two Gentlemen Ushers.

The Chief Mourner, Sir PETER PARKER, in a large mourning coach in which were Sir Thomas Williams and Sir Richard Keats, and Sir Edward Berry, and Sir F—— Blackwood, all in mourning cloaks, over their full uniform coats, their scarfs, breeches, and stockings, crape round their arms and hats.

Six Assistant Mourners, being Admirals (in two mourning coaches), in mourning cloaks, &c.

Banner of Emblems, in front of a mourning coach, in which were a Captain, and two Lieutenants, of the Royal Navy, as with the other Banners.

The Banner of Arms (in a mourning coach), in which were a Captain, and two Lieutenants, of the Royal Navy, as with the other Banners.

Officers of the Navy and Army, according to their respective ranks, the Seniors nearest the body.

The whole in fifty mourning coaches.

The private chariot of the deceased Lord—empty—the blinds drawn up—the coachman and footman in deep mourning, with bouquets of cypress.

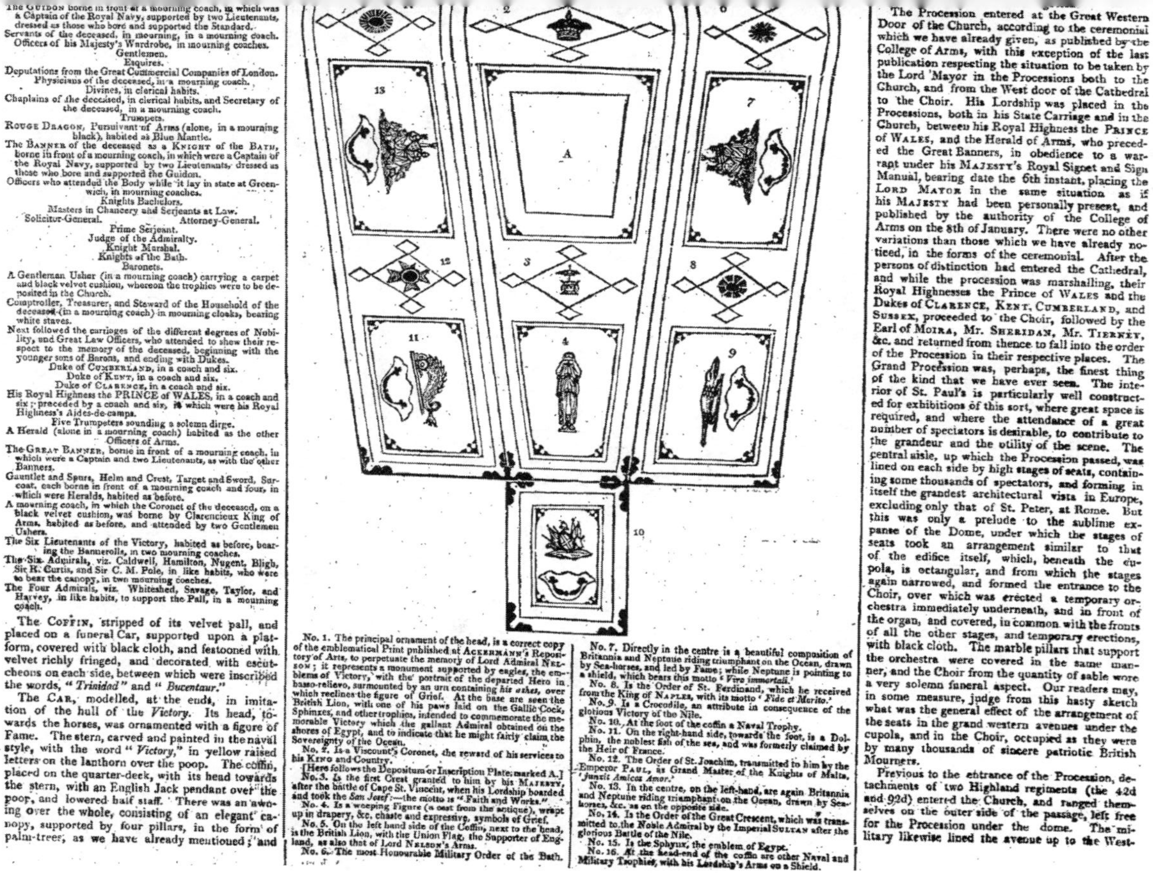

The Guidon borne in front of a mourning coach, in which was a Captain of the Royal Navy, supported by two Lieutenants, dressed as those who bore and supported the Standard.
Servants of the deceased, in mourning, in a mourning coach.
Officers of his Majesty's Wardrobe, in mourning coaches.
Gentlemen.
Esquires.
Deputations from the Great Commercial Companies of London.
Physicians of the deceased, in a mourning coach.
Divines, in clerical habits.
Chaplains of the deceased, in clerical habits, and Secretary of the deceased, in a mourning coach.
Trumpets.
Rouge Dragon, Pursuivant of Arms (alone, in a mourning black), habited as Blue Mantle.
The Banner of the deceased as a Knight of the Bath, borne in front of a mourning coach, in which were a Captain of the Royal Navy, supported by two Lieutenants, dressed as those who bore and supported the Guidon.
Officers who attended the Body while it lay in state at Greenwich, in mourning coaches.
Knights Bachelors.
Masters in Chancery and Serjeants at Law.
Solicitor-General. Attorney-General.
Prime Serjeant.
Judge of the Admiralty.
Knight Marshal.
Knights of the Bath.
Baronets.
A Gentleman Usher (in a mourning coach) carrying a carpet and black velvet cushion, whereon the trophies were to be deposited in the Church.
Comptroller, Treasurer, and Steward of the Household of the deceased (in a mourning coach) in mourning cloaks, bearing white staves.
Next followed the carriages of the different degrees of Nobility, and Great Law Officers, who attended to shew their respect to the memory of the deceased, beginning with the younger sons of Barons, and ending with Dukes.
Duke of Cumberland, in a coach and six.
Duke of Kent, in a coach and six.
Duke of Clarence, in a coach and six.
His Royal Highness the PRINCE of WALES, in a coach and six; preceded by a coach and six, in which were his Royal Highness's Aides-de-camps.
Five Trumpeters sounding a solemn dirge.
A Herald (alone in a mourning coach) habited as the other Officers of Arms.
The Great Banner, borne in front of a mourning coach, in which were a Captain and two Lieutenants, as with the other Banners.
Gauntlet and Spurs, Helm and Crest, Target and Sword, Surcoat, each borne in front of a mourning coach and four, in which were Heralds, habited as before.
A mourning coach, in which the Coronet of the deceased, on a black velvet cushion, was borne by Clarencieux King of Arms, habited as before, and attended by two Gentlemen Ushers.
The Six Lieutenants of the Victory, habited as before, bearing the Bannerolls, in two mourning coaches.
The Six Admirals, viz. Caldwell, Hamilton, Nugent, Bligh, Sir R. Curtis, and Sir C. M. Pole, in like habits, who were to bear the canopy, in two mourning coaches.
The Four Admirals, viz. Whiteshed, Savage, Taylor, and Harvey, in like habits, to support the Pall, in a mourning coach.

The Coffin, stripped of its velvet pall, and placed on a funeral Car, supported upon a platform, covered with black cloth, and festooned with velvet richly fringed, and decorated with escutcheons on each side, between which were inscribed the words, "*Trinidad*" and "*Bucentaur.*"

The Car, modelled, at the ends, in imitation of the hull of the *Victory*. Its head, towards the horses, was ornamented with a figure of Fame. The stern, carved and painted in the naval style, with the word "*Victory,*" in yellow raised letters on the lanthorn over the poop. The coffin, placed on the quarter-deck, with its head towards the stern, with an English Jack pendant over the poop, and lowered half staff. There was an awning over the whole, consisting of an elegant canopy, supported by four pillars, in the form of palm-trees, as we have already mentioned; and

No. 1. The principal ornament of the head, is a correct copy of the emblematical Print published at Ackermann's Repository of Arts, to perpetuate the memory of Lord Admiral Nelson; it represents a monument supported by eagles, the emblems of Victory, with the portrait of the departed Hero in basso-relievo, surmounted by an urn containing *his ashes*, over which reclines the figure of Grief. At the base are seen the British Lion, with one of his paws laid on the Gallic Cock, Sphinxes, and other trophies, intended to commemorate the memorable Victory which the gallant Admiral obtained on the shores of Egypt, and to indicate that he might fairly claim the Sovereignty of the Ocean.

No. 2. Is a Viscount's Coronet, the reward of his services to his King and Country.

[Here follows the Depositum or Inscription Plate, marked A.]

No. 3. Is the first Crest granted to him by his Majesty, after the battle of Cape St. Vincent, when his Lordship boarded and took the *San Josef*:—the motto is "Faith and Works."

No. 4. Is a weeping Figure (a cast from the antique), wrapt up in drapery, &c. chaste and expressive, symbols of Grief.

No. 5. On the left hand side of the Coffin, next to the head, is the British Lion, with the Union Flag, the Supporter of England, as also that of Lord Nelson's Arms.

No. 6. The most Honourable Military Order of the Bath.

No. 7. Directly in the centre is a beautiful composition of Britannia and Neptune riding triumphant on the Ocean, drawn by Sea-horses, and led by Fame; while Neptune is pointing to a shield, which bears this motto '*Viro immortali.*'

No. 8. Is the Order of St. Ferdinand, which he received from the King of Naples, with its motto '*Fide et Merito.*'

No. 9. Is a Crocodile, an attribute in consequence of the glorious Victory of the Nile.

No. 10. At the foot of the coffin a Naval Trophy.

No. 11. On the right-hand side, towards the foot, is a Dolphin, the noblest fish of the sea, and was formerly claimed by the Heir of France.

No. 12. The Order of St. Joachim, transmitted to him by the Emperor Paul, as Grand Master of the Knights of Malta, '*Junxit Amicos Amor.*'

No. 13. In the centre, on the left-hand, are again Britannia and Neptune riding triumphant on the Ocean, drawn by Sea-horses, &c. as on the opposite side.

No. 14. Is the Order of the Great Crescent, which was transmitted to the Noble Admiral by the Imperial Sultan after the glorious Battle of the Nile.

No. 15. Is the Sphynx, the emblem of Egypt.

No. 16. At the head-end of the coffin are other Naval and Military Trophies, with his Lordship's Arms on a Shield.

The Procession entered at the Great Western Door of the Church, according to the ceremonial which we have already given, as published by the College of Arms, with this exception of the last publication respecting the situation to be taken by the Lord Mayor in the Processions both to the Church, and from the West door of the Cathedral to the Choir. His Lordship was placed in the Processions, both in his State Carriage and in the Church, between his Royal Highness the Prince of Wales, and the Herald of Arms, who preceded the Great Banners, in obedience to a warrant under his Majesty's Royal Signet and Sign Manual, bearing date the 6th instant, placing the Lord Mayor in the same situation as if his Majesty had been personally present, and published by the authority of the College of Arms on the 8th of January. There were no other variations than those which we have already noticed, in the forms of the ceremonial. After the persons of distinction had entered the Cathedral, and while the procession was marshalling, their Royal Highnesses the Prince of Wales and the Dukes of Clarence, Kent, Cumberland, and Sussex, proceeded to the Choir, followed by the Earl of Moira, Mr. Sheridan, Mr. Tierney, &c. and returned from thence to fall into the order of the Procession in their respective places. The Grand Procession was, perhaps, the finest thing of the kind that we have ever seen. The interior of St. Paul's is particularly well constructed for exhibitions of this sort, where great space is required, and where the attendance of a great number of spectators is desirable, to contribute to the grandeur and the utility of the scene. The central aisle, up which the Procession passed, was lined on each side by high stages of seats, containing some thousands of spectators, and forming in itself the grandest architectural vista in Europe, excluding only that of St. Peter, at Rome. But this was only a prelude to the sublime expanse of the Dome, under which the stages of seats took an arrangement similar to that of the edifice itself, which, beneath the cupola, is octangular, and from which the stages again narrowed, and formed the entrance to the Choir, over which was erected a temporary orchestra immediately underneath, and in front of the organ, and covered, in common with the fronts of all the other stages, and temporary erections, with black cloth. The marble pillars that support the orchestra were covered in the same manner, and the Choir from the quantity of sable wore a very solemn funeral aspect. Our readers may, in some measure, judge from this hasty sketch what was the general effect of the arrangement of the seats in the grand western avenues under the cupola, and in the Choir, occupied as they were by many thousands of sincere patriotic British Mourners.

Previous to the entrance of the Procession, detachments of two Highland regiments (the 42d and 92d) entered the Church, and ranged themselves on the outer side of the passage, left free for the Procession under the dome. The military likewise lined the avenue up to the West-

Fig. 5.2. Nelson's funeral car and funeral casket. *The Times*, 10 November 1805.

by the issue of 22 June 1861, which contained 'no fewer than 24 pages, or 144 columns!'[10] 'If no waters nor mountains intervened, a column of *The Times* might be laid down almost half the distance to India', James Grant estimated, assuming that all 96 columns of 70,000 impressions were cut up into single columns. 'The Times may indeed be called the Monarch of the Press', Grant proclaimed. Yet even while its monarchy was being vaunted, it was already being overhauled in circulation.

Price cuts and Jumbo

The *Daily Telegraph* overtook *The Times* by means of two hard-sell tactics: price cuts on the one hand, and appeal to the middle classes on the other.

The *Daily Telegraph* started publication on 29 June 1855, under the title *Daily Telegraph and Courier*. It was a single sheet, price 2d (twopence). This was the cheapest paper, but 'notwithstanding that, it created no general interest',[11] and almost went bankrupt: '"How near . . . the public [was] of losing for ever a paper which has since ministered so much, and is doubtless destined to minister still more, for an indefinite time to come, to its enlightenment and gratification!"'[12] commented Grant.

Then the price was reduced to one penny, and 'This gave the circulation a powerful impulse.'[13] In the half-year ending 1870, it showed an average daily sale of almost 200,000. It was therefore 'justified in the statement which it makes of having "the largest newspaper circulation in the world"'.[14]

And then came Jumbo. 'In 1882 . . . the Daily
Telegraph stumbled across a journalistic crock of gold.
it was grey and enormous . . . This was Jumbo, already
the best-known animal in London Zoo.'[15]

The zoo had sold Jumbo to Barnum, the American
circus owner, and he was led away from his supposed
'wife' Alice to Millwall Docks. According to the *Daily
Telegraph* reporter: 'The poor brute moaned sadly, . . .
embracing the man [his keeper] with his trunk, and
actually kneeling before him. Jumbo's cries were soon
heard in the elephant house, where poor Alice was
again seized with alarm and grief.'[16] Eventually, Jumbo
was led back, 'and the joy of Alice knew no bounds,
her delights being expressed with clumsy gambols
round her compartment'.[17]

But there was no need to feel sorry for Alice, his
supposed mate: they never did share a cage, and the
Jumbo–Alice romance was a journalistic invention.
Jumbo did kneel down, but this was due to a serious
long-standing knee problem.

In spite of the outcry, Jumbo was eventually
taken off to America, where in 1885 he was killed by a
freight train as he was being led across a railway line.
'Both train and Jumbo were wrecked',[18] as Matthew
Engel observed.

A plethora of papers

The Times and the *Telegraph* were not the only
nineteenth-century broadsheets: the *Manchester
Guardian* was founded in 1821, and a more downmarket
paper, the *Daily Mail*, in 1896. The *News of the World*

first appeared on 1 October 1843, though it would be unrecognizable to today's reading public. Its front page, like that of other newspapers, was a dense mass of small print.

A plethora of other newspapers, both morning and evening, were published at the end of the nineteenth century. In a story first published in 1892, the fictional detective Sherlock Holmes needed to find a particular witness in London: '"To do this, we must try the simplest means first, and these lie undoubtedly in an advertisement in all the evening papers . . . in the *Globe, Star, Pall Mall, St. James's, Evening News Standard, Echo,* and any others that occur to you"'.[19]

But even more notable than the plethora of papers was the continued downmarket trend. Entertainment increasingly pushed aside more serious news. In 1896 the *Daily Telegraph* 'was in turn overwhelmed by the *Daily Mail*, which was beaten by the *Daily Express*, which was beaten by the *Daily Mirror*, which was beaten by *The Sun*'.[20]

Tickling the public

> Tickle the public, make 'em grin,
> The more you tickle, the more you'll win;
> Teach the public, you'll never get rich,
> You'll live like a beggar and die in a ditch.

This anonymous verse went round Fleet Street in the nineteenth century.[21] Newspapers have to 'tickle' readers, otherwise nobody would buy them, as Samuel Keimer, a religious eccentric, discovered in the early nineteenth century, when he launched the

Pennsylvania Gazette in America. His definition of
'news' was narrow and high-minded: 'We have
little News of Consequence at present, the English
Prints being generally stufft with Robberies, Cheats,
Fires, Murders, Bankruptcies, Promotions of some, and
Hangings of others.'[22] He made this complaint in his
first issue. To counteract this seeming lack of news, he
offered his readers an extract from an encyclopaedia:
'In the mean Time we hope our Readers will be content for the present, with what we can give 'em, which
if it does 'em no Good, shall do 'em no Hurt. 'Tis the
best we have, and so take it.' But lively news is essential, if readers are to be attracted and maintained.

The word *news* originally meant 'new events'
(chapter 4), and still does, according to recent dictionaries: 'News: Information . . . about important or
interesting recent events'.[23] Yet this definition is only
partially true of the content of modern newspapers,
where, increasingly, 'News is anything that makes a
reader say "Gee Whiz!"'[24] More realistically, perhaps,
'News is simply what made it into today's paper or
news broadcast.'[25] And what makes it into newspapers
has to make an impact.

Any attempt to shock typically meets with
disapproval: 'An outcry of literary men is raised against
sensationalism', noted Henry Labouchere, founder in
1877 of a gossipy paper, *Truth*, in America, but, as he
pointed out, 'it is the business of newspapers to create
a sensation'.[26]

But this raises a query: if newspapers are trying
to boggle the mind, are they reporting events, or
providing a biased selection?

'Have you noticed that life, real honest-to-goodness life, with murders and catastrophes and fabulous inheritances, happens almost exclusively in newspapers?'[27] said the dramatist Jean Anouilh. Disasters, deaths and conflicts are the 'bread-and-butter' of newspapers, especially on front pages: 'If it bleeds, it leads' is an old journalistic adage. 'Get me a murder a day!' is a motto attributed to Lord Northcliffe, founder of the *Daily Mail*. A retired reporter reminisces about old times: 'There's the telephone ringing. "Hullo, hullo!" calls a sub-editor quietly. "Who are you? Margate mystery? Go ahead. They've found the corpse? All right. Keep it to a column, but send a good story. Horrible mutilations? Good. Glimpse the corpse yourself if you can. Yes,
send full mutilations. Will call for them at eleven. Good-bye"'.[28]

People often claim to be disgusted and upset by newspaper coverage, yet are often avid devourers of shock-horror reports. In his verse 'A ballad for breakfast time' (1931),[29] the comic-poet A. P. Herbert begins by expressing dismay at the content of morning papers:

> There's not very much in the paper,
>   But what's in the paper is bad,
> A peeress has married a draper,
>   An aeroplane's crashed in Bagdad.
> A girl has been cruelly battered,
>   She was battered to death with a bat . . .
> News! News! It gives you the blues . . .
> Why do we peruse the discouraging news
>   On a mouldy Monday morning?

But by the last verse, the newspaper reader has become addicted to the drama:

Dramas, pyjamas and drugs and booze,
Arsons and parsons and all their views,
Smashes and crashes that don't amuse! . . .
But meanwhile I glues my nose to the news
  Every mouldy morning.

And a verse published in the *New Clarion* (1932), to the tune of 'Drunken sailor'[30] makes a similar point:

What shall we put in the daily paper?
Suicide of linen draper,
Duchess poisoned by noxious vapour,
Early in the morning.
Awful international crisis,
Idiot reader wins three prizes,
See how the British public rises
Early in the morning.

Yet shock-horror stories alone are not enough. They have to be tied in with other criteria for newsworthiness, as will be outlined below.

Newsworthy news

A dramatic event cannot be the only reason for including something in a newspaper or television bulletin. If drama was the only requirement, then the death of Cleopatra or Julius Caesar from centuries ago could be endlessly re-reported. The criteria used by reporters to include or exclude something as 'news' are therefore of interest. To some extent 'newsworthiness' varies from decade to decade and from country to country. On closer inspection, the notion is a complex one which needs to be teased apart.[31]

A now classic article was written in 1965 by
two Scandinavians, Johan Galtung and Mari Holmboe
Ruge, who initially tried to identify news values for
foreign news in the Scandinavian press. Their insightful conclusions have made their work a starting point
for those considering the topic of newsworthiness. As
they point out, 'we cannot register everything, we
have to select, and the question is what will strike our
attention'.[32] Events become news, they suggest, to the
extent that they satisfy certain conditions. They list
a number of relevant factors, which are not necessarily independent, but tend to follow certain
patterns of intertwining. Later researchers have built
on their work, and proposed further criteria. The
following is a shortish list summarizing what is
often these days deemed newsworthy.

Recency is essential: anything that happened
much more than twenty-four hours ago is unlikely to
be 'news'. As the journalist Andrew Marr points out:
'One moment news is verbal diamonds, the next it
is dust. It seems in this respect like a drug . . . a
brief verbal flurry in the brain, then just a dirty
smudge'.[33]

Proximity also matters: 'Small earthquake in Chile:
not many dead' is a well-known spoof example of
'non-news', partly because Chile is far away, and also
because the earthquake was a small one. 'A whole
population might be destroyed in Peking or Macedonia,
but it would not interest them [uneducated readers]
as much as a fight in a street in which their aunt
once lived!' it has been claimed.[34]

Negativity also has a high priority: bad news is more newsworthy than good news. 'What's in the paper is bad', as A. P. Herbert expressed it, in his 'Ballad for breakfast time', quoted on pp. 86–7. Further lines in this run:

> Our trade is deplorably groggy,
>   A bad epidemic is near,
> The forecast is 'Freezing and Foggy,'
>   They think you get cancer from beer . . .
> News! News! It gives you the blues,
>   Sinners and winners and why they lose;
> But everyone chews his bit of bad news
>   On a mouldy Monday morning.

Negativity ties in with unexpectedness, usually a shocking sudden event. Together, negativity and unexpectedness create the 'shock-horror' effect required to capture people's attention. And interest in extreme events is a sign of a healthy, well-adjusted society. As Andrew Marr points out: 'But journalism which did not find murder interesting would represent a fantastically violent society. Murder is extreme behaviour; and all extreme behaviour is interesting to those who live in the tepid middle of things.'[35]

Person-centredness is also important, and explains why mega-tragedies are often illustrated by the highlighting of one particular victim, or victims' abandoned possessions.

These days, television enthrals viewers with its walking and talking illustrations of shock-horror events. Consequently, in newspapers, the appetite for dramatic, recent and proximate stories has been equalled, and in some papers overtaken, by an obsession with gossip and celebrities.

The chat of the day

A desire for chit-chat and scandal is one of long standing. Ben Jonson's play *Staple of news* (1626) featured an imaginary news agency, where the employees are instructed to gather gossip:

> Sirs,
> You must get o'this news . . .
> Who dines and sups i'the town, where and with whom.[36]

In the early eighteenth century, Daniel Defoe, the author of *Robinson Crusoe*, launched a serious *Review*, with the aim of explaining what was happening in Europe. At the end, he added a prototype gossip column: 'After our serious matters are over, we shall at the end of every paper present you with a little diversion, as anything occurs to make the world merry.'[37] This 'diversion' covered 'such vices as duelling, swearing, and the lustful and drunken escapades of the clergy'.

Towards the end of the eighteenth century, Richard Sheridan's play *The school for scandal* (1777) began with Lady Sneerwell checking that the scandalmonger Snake has, as requested, inserted false gossip into a publication:

LADY SNEERWELL. The paragraphs, you say, Mr. Snake, were all inserted?

SNAKE. They were, madam, and as I copied them myself in a feigned hand, there can be no suspicion whence they came.

LADY SNEERWELL. Did you circulate the report of Lady
    Brittle's intrigue with Captain Boastall?
SNAKE. That's in as fine a train as your ladyship could
    wish.[38]

In the late eighteenth century, newspapers
routinely began to print items on social habits or
fashion, possibly aiming to entice readers who
previously had found such fare in magazines. The
writer Charles Lamb reminisced about how he
had been employed by the *Morning Post*:

In those days every Morning Paper . . . kept an author, who
was bound to furnish daily a quantum of witty paragraphs.
Sixpence a joke . . . The chat of the day, scandal, but above
all, *dress*, furnished the material. The length of no paragraph
was to exceed seven lines . . .
    A fashion of *flesh*, or rather *pink*-coloured hose for
the ladies luckily coming up at this juncture . . . We were
pronounced a 'capital hand'.[39]

Later, he began to find this a chore: 'It was not every
week that a fashion of pink stockings came up; but
mostly, instead of it, some rugged intractable subject;
some topic impossible to be contorted into the risible.'
    As the decades rolled on, gossip increasingly vied
with serious news stories. Evelyn Waugh's novel *Vile
bodies* (1930) features two young aristocratic journalists,
named as the fifteenth Marquess of Vanburgh and the
eighth Earl of Balcairn, gathering details of the latest
society party for their readers, and discussing their
work:

'Hello' he said. 'Isn't this a repulsive party? What are
you going to say about it?' . . . 'I've just telephoned my story
through,' said Lord Balcairn. 'And now I'm going, thank God.'

'I can't think of what to say,' said Lord Vanburgh. 'My editress said yesterday she was tired of seeing the same names over and over again – and here they are again, all of them.'[40]

The Second World War (1939–45) brought non-serious journalism to a temporary halt. When newsprint shortages eased, society gossip competed with trivia from the entertainment industry: Lord Beaverbrook 'was the first Fleet Street mogul to understand that the kind of froth that bubbled . . . especially from Hollywood – would sell more newspapers than any amount of hard news coverage or political acumen'.[41] And this trend continued.

Gossip guzzlers

'We are all gossip guzzlers now . . . gossip has become a sulphurous brew that has long since burst the confines of traditional gossip columns and cascades over the daily newspaper diet of millions',[42] comments Roger Wilkes, in a book called *Scandal*. Yet what is new is not so much the inclusion of gossip, as its quantity, the avalanche of trivia which these days threatens to bury serious news stories.

'Gossip curdled in the 1970s',[43] comments Wilkes. By the end of the decade, it had moved from the inside or back to the front pages, 'offering an increasingly star-struck readership a bewildering array of incon-sequential stories about equally inconsequential people all jostling for attention in Fleet Street's new "popocracy"'.[44]

'The tabloids sagged with increasingly intrusive stories and pictures about . . . celebrities who were

"known for their well-knownness'",[45] Wilkes
comments. If a genuine celebrity marries, or dies,
the coverage can be overwhelming, spilling over even
into the broadsheets. When George Harrison, a former
member of the pop-group, the Beatles, died of cancer
in November 2001, the entire British press cleared their
front pages, and many more inside, for an appreciation
'on a scale that, only a few years ago, would have
been reserved for the Second Coming' (of Christ).[46]

'So gossip gurgles on', and 'has overtaken news on
the tabloid agenda; . . . [with people] looking to their
newspapers for entertainment rather than information'.[47] As Wilkes notes: 'We no longer seem to care too
much for the real world, with its trials and tribula-
tions. It seems we would rather be poking our noses
into other people's business, truffling for that juicy
morsel of gossip and scandal. And the more we
uncover, it seems the louder we clamour for
more.'[48]

Bloated boobs

This trend has continued, with increasing quantities
of tittle-tattle about celebrities, their love affairs and
their appearance. Not long ago, a tabloid devoted the
main story on its front page to opinions about a
celebrity's breast structure:

The verdict is in – Posh's boobs are FAKE. Brits reckon by a
landslide majority that Victoria Beckham's cleavage is
man-made.
   A bouncing 72% of voters said they thought Posh's breasts
were not real. Only one in five people thought her stunning

chest was the work of Mother Nature and a well-engineered Bra.[49]

On the centre page spread, more bulging boobs were highlighted, with the header 'Real or Fake?' under the strapline: 'How to tell the naturally talented from the silicone sizzlers'.

On the same day, another tabloid highlighted as its main story an argument between celebrities over hair-styles:

Victoria Beckham had her brunette locks dyed blonde yesterday – but told hairdressers: 'Don't make me look like that dog Jordan.'

Posh, 29, stepped up their bitter feud as she spent £1,300 on highlights and hair extensions at the same North London salon used by the 25-year-old glamour model.[50]

Readers could get the impression that the whole world is composed of celebrity trivia. The first edition of the *News of the World* had as its front page lead one Sunday: 'My wild sex with Sven'[51] – an account of a sexual affair between the English football coach and his secretary. A second edition of the same newspaper had as its lead story: 'I bedded Sven and his boss'. The lady in question had claimed Sven was not her only bedfellow, and the newspaper (presumably) felt this item of information would sell more newspapers, and altered the front page accordingly.

Meanwhile, the type of story which might one day have made the front page in such a paper was relegated to page 43 – 'Runaway car kills tot on beach' ran the headline, above the first paragraph: 'A two-year-old boy was crushed to death last night when a

runaway car plunged 12ft from a seafront car park
to the beach below.'

Perhaps the *News of the World* did not want to
upset its readers with tragedy on a Sunday. Or perhaps
the comic poet Ogden Nash summed up the trend for
gossipy trivia best, when he wrote:

> There are two kinds of people who blow through life like a
> breeze,
> And one kind is gossipers, and the other kind is gossipees.
> And they certainly annoy each other.
> But they certainly enjoy each other.
> But they couldn't do without each other.[52]

Yet gossip about celebrities is not necessarily bad.
The media these days is – perhaps rightly – partly
concerned with making people feel that they belong in
their culture, and maybe could make a contribution.
As Andrew Marr points out: 'A celebrity culture . . .
may be shallow . . . but it is open to anyone with the
looks and the luck to join in.'[53] Or, as a psychologist
has suggested, celebrity biographies 'act as modern
fairytales, showing us how to overcome hardship and
pave the way to success. Seeing celebrities talk about
coping with life situations which mirror our own
can act as a stimulus to help us open up.'[54]

This chapter has looked at the emergence of daily
newspapers, and the way in which they interleave hard
news with an increasing quantity of gossip. The next
chapter will explore how journalists structure their
stories.

CHAPTER SIX

Story-telling

Narrating the news

Journalists are professional story-tellers of our age. The fairy
tale starts: 'Once upon a time.' The news story begins:
'Fifteen people were injured today when a bus plunged . . .'

Allan Bell, The language of news media (1991)[1]

Modern newspapers continue a long-standing
tradition of story-telling, handed down from one era
to another. Traditional bards (chapter 2) passed it onto
ballad-mongers, chapbooks and newsbooks (chapter 4).
In the nineteenth and twentieth centuries,
newspapers took over.

Accounts of the murder of two ten-year-old children
at Soham, England, in August 2002, continued this
tradition, as a writer for *The Times* pointed out: 'Murder
stories have always dominated popular culture through
folk songs, "penny dreadfuls", chap-books and
ballads . . . Tales of the slaying of innocent children or
fair maidens were particularly prized. Soham fitted the
pattern perfectly with the ghastly added twists of a
double murder and paedophilia.'[2] A television film

of these events was a 21st-century *True Chronicle of the Most Horrible Murders Lately Perpetrated at Soham*, he suggested.

Such accounts are carefully crafted: 'Journalists . . . write stories. A story has structure, direction, point, viewpoint',[3] as Allan Bell, himself once a journalist, points out.

News stories have their own conventions. When these are broken, the result is likely to be an unreadable hotch-potch, perhaps similar to the efforts of Boot, a fictional would-be journalist in Evelyn Waugh's novel *Scoop* (1938). Boot is a nature-lover who pens a bi-weekly half-column for a newspaper: 'Feather-footed through the plashy fen passes the questing vole . . .'[4] He is mistaken for a top journalist and sent to a world trouble spot. His heart heavy with misgiving, Boot types the first news report of his career:

NOTHING MUCH HAS HAPPENED EXCEPT TO THE PRESIDENT WHO HAS BEEN IMPRISONED IN HIS OWN PALACE BY REVOLUTIONARY JUNTA HEADED BY SUPERIOR BLACK CALLED BENITO AND RUSSIAN JEW WHO BANNISTER SAYS IS NO GOOD THEY SAY HE IS DRUNK WHEN CHILDREN TRY TO SEE HIM BUT GOVERNESS SAYS MOST UNUSUAL LOVELY SPRING WEATHER BUBONIC PLAGUE RAGING.[5]

Compare this with a typical news story in a modern paper. Under a headline 'Moscow disaster kills 13', the bare bones of the story are neatly summarized at the beginning of the news report: 'At least 13 people, including two children, died and more than 90 were injured when the glass roof over a swimming pool

Fig. 6.1. Moscow swimming pool disaster, *The Times*, 5 February 2004.

at a leisure centre on the outskirts of Moscow collapsed yesterday.'[6]

This is typical of a modern, competent story, where all the vital information is crammed in early.

Who? What? Where? How? Why? When?

> I keep six honest serving-men
> (They taught me all I knew);
> Their names are What and Why and When
> And How and Where and Who.

These lines, from Rudyard Kipling's 'Just-So' story 'The elephant's child',[7] contain the same six words, 'five W's and an H', with which journalists are taught to start newspaper reports: 'Think of it as a silent chant: Who-What-How? Why-When-Where?'[8] advises one manual for trainees. The W/H words signal the key points of every news story: WHO was involved? WHAT happened? WHERE did it happen? HOW did it happen? WHY did it happen? WHEN did it happen?

The journalist's W/H words are not all equally important. *Who*, *what* and *where* are crucial. *How* is moderately important. *Why* is not always known. *When* is often unnecessary, because if this is real 'news', that is, new events, then it has probably only just happened. Skilled journalists pack all the vital information into a single sentence. The report might be about a major disaster: 'More than 200 people were killed yesterday when runaway train wagons laden with fuel and chemicals exploded after being derailed in northeast Iran.'[9]

Or it could outline a single person's misfortune: 'A pensioner died yesterday after being dragged from his car, robbed and beaten when he stopped to ask for directions yesterday morning.'[10]

Or it might be a story whose outcome is as yet unknown: 'Cops have called in computer experts to find a schoolgirl they fear is in the clutches of an internet chatroom fiend.'[11]

But news reports contain more than a succinct first sentence. The events are presented with the most recent at the beginning. Below this, the whole story has been carefully structured, as will be outlined below.

Ordering the order of events

Up until the turn of the twentieth century, newspapers, like their predecessors the newsbooks (chapter 4), recounted events in the order in which they occurred, as in the following account in the London *Times* (1 September 1888) of one of the crimes committed in London's East End by the notorious nineteenth-century murderer known as 'Jack the Ripper'.[12] The newspaper report has the sober headline ANOTHER MURDER IN WHITECHAPEL. The article, which is over 1,000 words long, is crushed into two long dense paragraphs, though, for readability, these have been split up in the abridged version given below:

Another murder of the foulest kind was committed in the neighbourhood of Whitechapel in the early hours of

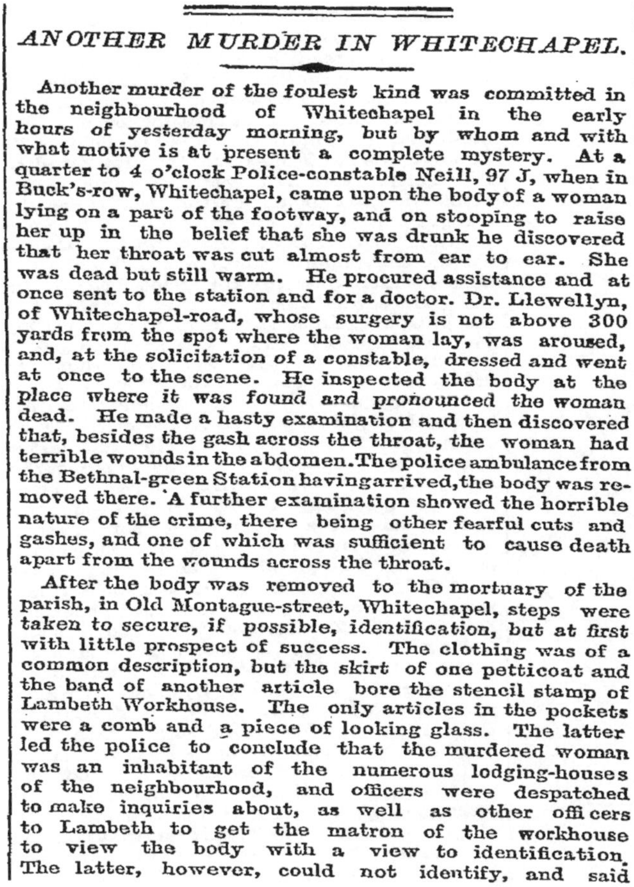

ANOTHER MURDER IN WHITECHAPEL.

Another murder of the foulest kind was committed in the neighbourhood of Whitechapel in the early hours of yesterday morning, but by whom and with what motive is at present a complete mystery. At a quarter to 4 o'clock Police-constable Neill, 97 J, when in Buck's-row, Whitechapel, came upon the body of a woman lying on a part of the footway, and on stooping to raise her up in the belief that she was drunk he discovered that her throat was cut almost from ear to ear. She was dead but still warm. He procured assistance and at once sent to the station and for a doctor. Dr. Llewellyn, of Whitechapel-road, whose surgery is not above 300 yards from the spot where the woman lay, was aroused, and, at the solicitation of a constable, dressed and went at once to the scene. He inspected the body at the place where it was found and pronounced the woman dead. He made a hasty examination and then discovered that, besides the gash across the throat, the woman had terrible wounds in the abdomen. The police ambulance from the Bethnal-green Station having arrived, the body was removed there. A further examination showed the horrible nature of the crime, there being other fearful cuts and gashes, and one of which was sufficient to cause death apart from the wounds across the throat.

After the body was removed to the mortuary of the parish, in Old Montague-street, Whitechapel, steps were taken to secure, if possible, identification, but at first with little prospect of success. The clothing was of a common description, but the skirt of one petticoat and the band of another article bore the stencil stamp of Lambeth Workhouse. The only articles in the pockets were a comb and a piece of looking glass. The latter led the police to conclude that the murdered woman was an inhabitant of the numerous lodging-houses of the neighbourhood, and officers were despatched to make inquiries about, as well as other officers to Lambeth to get the matron of the workhouse to view the body with a view to identification. The latter, however, could not identify, and said

Fig. 6.2. ANOTHER MURDER IN WHITECHAPEL, *The Times*, 1 September 1888.

that the clothing might have been issued any time during the past two or three years. As the news of the murder spread, however, first one woman and then another came forward to view the body, and at length it was found that a woman answering the description of the murdered woman had lodged in a common lodging-house, 18, Thrawl-street, Spitalfields. Women from that place were fetched and they identified the deceased as " Polly," who had shared a room with three other women in the place on the usual terms of such houses —nightly payment of 4d. each, each woman having a separate bed. It was gathered that the deceased had led the life of an " unfortunate " while lodging in the house, which was only for about three weeks past. Nothing more was known of her by them but that when she presented herself for her lodging on Thursday night she was turned away by the deputy because she had not the money. She was then the worse for drink, but not drunk, and turned away laughing, saying, " I'll soon get my ' doss ' money ; see what a jolly bonnet I've got now." She was wearing a bonnet which she had not been seen with before, and left the lodging-house door. A woman of the neighbourhood saw her later she told the police—even as late as 2 30 on Friday morning—in Whitechapel-road, opposite the church and at the corner of Osborne-street, and at a quarter to 4 she was found within 500 yards of the spot, murdered. The people of the lodging-house knew her as " Polly," but at about half-past 7 last evening a woman named Mary Ann Monk, at present an inmate of Lambeth Workhouse, was taken to the mortuary and identified the body as that of Mary Ann Nicholls, also called " Polly " Nicholls. She knew her, she said, as they were inmates of the Lambeth Workhouse together in April and May last, the deceased having been passed there from another workhouse. On the 12th of May, according to Monk, Nicholls left the workhouse to take a situation as servant at Ingleside, Wandsworth-common. It afterwards became known that Nicholls betrayed her trust as domestic servant, by stealing £3 from her employer and absconding. From that time she had been wandering about. Monk met her, she said, about six weeks ago when herself out of the workhouse and drank

Fig. 6.2. (*Cont.*)

with her. She was sure the deceased was "Polly" Nicholls, and, having twice viewed the features as the body lay in a shell, maintained her opinion. So far the police have satisfied themselves, but as to getting a clue to her murderer they express little hope. The matter is being investigated by Detective-inspector Abberline, of Scotland-yard, and Inspector Helson, J Division. The latter states that he walked carefully over the ground soon after 8 o'clock in the morning, and beyond the discolourations ordinarily found on pavements there was no sign of stains. Viewing the spot where the body was found, however, it seemed difficult to believe that the woman received her death wounds there. The police have no theory with respect to the matter, except that a gang of ruffians exists in the neighbourhood, which, blackmailing women of the "unfortunate" class, takes vengeance on those who do not find money for them. They base that surmise on the fact that within 12 months two other women have been murdered in the district by almost similar means—one as recently as the 6th of August last—and left in the gutter of the street in the early hours of the morning. If the woman was murdered on the spot where the body was found, it is almost impossible to believe she would not have aroused the neighbourhood by her screams, Bucks-row being a street tenanted all down one side by a respectable class of people, superior to many of the surrounding streets, the other side having a blank wall bounding a warehouse. Dr. Llewellyn has called the attention of the police to the smallness of the quantity of blood on the spot where he saw the body, and yet the gashes in the abdomen laid the body right open. The weapon used would scarcely have been a sailor's jack knife, but a pointed weapon with a stout back—such as a cork-cutter's or shoemaker's knife. In his opinion it was not an exceptionally long-bladed weapon. He does not believe that the woman was seized from behind and her throat cut, but thinks that a hand was held across her mouth and the knife then used, possibly by a left-handed man, as the bruising on the face of the deceased is such as would result from the mouth being covered with the right hand. He made a second examination of the body in the mortuary, and on that based his conclusion, but will make no actual *post mortem* until he receives the Coroner's orders. The inquest is fixed for to-day.

Fig. 6.2. (*Cont.*)

yesterday morning, but by whom and with what motive is at present a complete mystery.

At a quarter to 4 o'clock Police-constable Neill, 97 J, when in Buck's-row, Whitechapel, came upon the body of a woman lying on a part of the footway, and on stooping to raise her up in the belief that she was drunk he discovered that her throat was cut almost from ear to ear. She was dead but still warm. He procured assistance and at once sent to the station and for a doctor.

Dr. Llewellyn, of Whitechapel-road, whose surgery is not above 300 yards from the spot where the woman lay, was aroused, and, at the solicitation of a constable, dressed and went at once to the scene. He inspected the body at the place where it was found and pronounced the woman dead. He made a hasty examination and then discovered that, besides the gash across the throat, the woman had terrible wounds in the abdomen. The police ambulance from the Bethnal-green Station having arrived, the body was removed there. A further examination showed the horrible nature of the crime, there being other fearful cuts and gashes, and one of which was sufficient to cause death apart from the wounds across the throat.

After the body was removed to the mortuary of the parish, in Old-Montague-street, Whitechapel, steps were taken to secure, if possible, identification, but at first with little prospect of success . . . As the news of the murder spread, however, first one woman and then another came forward to view the body, and at length it was found that a woman answering the description of the murdered woman had lodged in a common lodging-house, 18, Thrawl-street, Spitalfields.

Women from that place were fetched and they identified the deceased as 'Polly', but at about half-past 7 last evening a woman named Mary Ann Monk . . . identified the body as that of May Ann Nicholls, also called 'Polly' Nicholls.

She knew her, she said, as they were inmates of the Lambeth Workhouse together in April and May last.

This old order-of-events account contrasts strikingly with the story structure typically found in modern-day newspapers.

Modern story structure

In a typical modern-day news story, the earliest of a whole sequence of episodes often comes almost at the end, as in a report of a car accident in the *Guardian*.[13] Here, the most recent event is placed at the beginning:

> Police officers pushed a note through a distraught husband's door asking him if he was going to collect his wife's crashed car without realising she was lying dead inside.
>
> Les London spent 36 hours searching for his estranged wife Sally, aged 39, after she failed to arrive at his home on Tuesday night.
>
> After reading the note Mr. London phoned police to say she was missing, and officers went back to the car to discover her body still inside.
>
> Police yesterday refused to say how their officers missed the body when they attended the scene of the crash on Wednesday morning.
>
> Mr. London, aged 49, sobbed outside his home in Lidlington, Beds, as he said: 'How could this have happened? I just want her back, but I know I can't have her.' Mrs. London's black Ford Capri is thought to have crashed on Tuesday night. It was found on its roof in a cornfield close to Ridgmont, Bedfordshire. Next morning, police saw the car but after failing to discover the driver, they stuck a 'Police Aware' notice on the vehicle and left.
>
> A spokesman for Bedfordshire police said a full inquiry was being launched.

The actual sequence of events, with P (paragraph) numbers of the report noted at the end of each event, was as follows:

1 Mrs. London crashes her car on Tuesday night (P 5).
2 Mr. London spends 36 hours searching for his wife (P 2).
3 Police find a car on its roof in a cornfield, and stick a 'Police Aware' notice on it (P 5).
4 Police push a note through Mr. London's door, asking him if he is planning to collect his crashed car (P 1).
5 Mr. London reads note, and phones police to say his wife is missing (P 3).
6 Police return to car, and discover Mrs. London's body inside (P 3).
7 Mr. London asks how this could have happened (P 5).
8 Police say an enquiry is being launched (P 6).

This car-crash account has been carefully organized, in a structure known as an 'inverted pyramid', basically an upside-down triangle. This is possibly the commonest of several ways of organizing a story. An initial summary comes at the top of the report. This outlines the most recent and most newsworthy event. Earlier events are then fitted in, in a way which progressively explains the situation. Each subsequent piece of information is assumed to be less important, and is given less space. Finally, an evaluation or summing up is presented, though this is not crucial to the story, and could have been omitted, if space had been short. The evaluation is likely to be a 'Watch this space' line such as 'Detectives are continuing to investigate', or 'The case is expected to come to trial early next year', maybe tempting the reader to buy further copies of the paper to follow up on the story. The broad overall structure is shown in Fig. 6.3.[14]

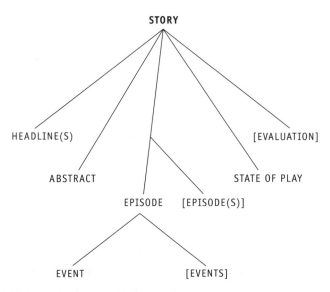

Fig. 6.3. Newspaper story structure.

At first sight, this structure seems like a specialized journalistic confection, which in some ways it is. But in other ways, it fits in with general expectations about the patterns of non-fiction. Some interesting similarities are found between the way a journalistic account is produced, and the way an academic article is structured.

ACADEMIC ARTICLE	VS	NEWSPAPER ARTICLE
TITLE		HEADLINE
SUBTITLE		SUB-HEAD
ABSTRACT		'ABSTRACT'
(above article)		(first sentence) wh × 6
EVIDENCE		EPISODE/EVENTS
RESULTS		STATE OF PLAY
CONCLUSION		[EVALUATION]

In news stories, the main advantage of the inverted pyramid structure is that someone perusing a paper in a hurry can simply stop after the first paragraph, knowing they have the basic outline: 'An RAF jet carrying the Prince of Wales came within seconds of colliding with a commercial airliner with 186 passengers on board after an air traffic control mix up.'[15] A casual reader probably would not want to spend more time on this 'non-story'. Nothing happened. Both planes were safe, as well as their passengers. The height of the jets, how far they were apart, and where Prince Charles and the other plane were going are optional extras which anyone interested in the details could find out further down the page, if they wanted to continue reading.

The 'inverted pyramid' structure is drummed into all trainee journalists, though it is not without problems. For a start, it is not always clear which facts are more important than others. After the initial summary, the ideal way of expanding and explaining might vary from reporter to reporter, or from reader to reader. So after the first sentence, the remainder of the piece might resemble a triple- or quadruple-decker sandwich, rather more than an upside-down triangle.

Many journalists therefore, especially those with experience, adapt the inverted pyramid in ways which suit their story. One variant is an 'hour-glass' structure.[16] This begins with an inverted pyramid, then at some point moves to a chronological survey of the facts. This has the advantage of clarifying the details in a complex story.

The so-called 'focus' style is another commonly found method of organization,[17] often favoured in feature articles. This approach focuses on a single person or situation which may not by itself be of great interest, but which is an example of a newsworthy problem. The story typically starts with, say, a pensioner who has lost his or her savings through the incompetence of a big organization, or someone whose health has been ruined by a hospital mishap. Then it moves on to the larger, more serious issues, which the misfortune of the individual illustrates. Finally, it typically moves back to the person whose plight was first highlighted, and updates the readers on his or her progress.

An example of this was an article on skin cancer called 'The burning issue' in a Sunday supplement.[18] It began with an account of a young woman who had regularly taken holidays in the sun. Her boyfriend noticed an unfamiliar mark on her toe, which turned out to be a malignant melanoma, a serious form of skin cancer. This led on to a general discussion of this type of cancer, and introduced facts and figures: 70,000 cases of skin cancer are reported each year, of which 7,000 are malignant and 1,600 fatal. Interviews with a consultant dermatologist and an information manager at Cancer Research UK followed, before a return to the original victim, who had recovered her health, and changed her ways: she 'went on holiday to Sardinia, and sat under a parasol, where she had time to reflect . . . Sometimes she applies fake tan from a plastic tube, and says she has just as good a time as she had before she became unwell.'

One little shoe

But story organization involves more than making decisions about the story structure. A good journalist tries to strike a balance between globally relevant matters and individual concerns, as in the 'burning issue' discussed above. 'A major air-crash, for example, is routinely reported as an event worthy of world-wide notice, while at the same time reporters try to make the tragedy vivid by highlighting the fate of innocent individuals: "one little shoe is all that was left of flight 999" is a journalistic cliché.'[19]

The juxtaposing of momentous, globally significant events with details of personal tragedies is found again and again. An avalanche in the French Alps killed numerous holiday-makers. Immediately afterwards, their personal possessions are described: 'Lying around the site were everyday objects: a single red ski boot, a child's comic, the libretto from *Rigoletto*, chairs, a glossy science magazine. I picked up someone's rent record. Beneath it was a toy car.'[20] A massacre of eight tourists in Bwindi, Uganda, highlighted the pitiful scattered remnants of their lives: 'poignant reminders of the ordinariness of the lives that had been shattered included a fixture list for Wolverhampton Wanderers, the stub of a ticket to see Shakespeare in Love and a cassette of music by Crowded House. On the path leading to the hills were a single boot and a plastic shoe.'[21] An earthquake in Turkey caused a tidal wave which drowned numerous victims. Reminders of normal life are spotted beneath the water: 'The rubble of a block of holiday flats leaves everyday reminders of the thousands of lives lost – a child's teddy, its fur gently swaying in the current; a clock stopped at 3.02am; chess pieces; a bar of foaming soap.'[22] These accounts were typical, yet dwarfed by the reports of the Asian tsunami disaster (December 2004). Paper after paper carried brutal, opening paragraphs, describing the tragedy, followed by individual stories of suffering and/or survival, as in the following:

> Tidal waves that carried terror to the coastlines of seven countries had claimed 12,000 lives last night.
> Thousands more were missing feared dead after a massive undersea earthquake sent a wall of water thundering across the Indian Ocean.
> The waves 30 ft high and travelling faster than 300mph at their worst, smashed into coastlines thousands of miles apart, washing away whole villages and dragging sunbathers and snorkellers out to sea.[23]

Further on in the article, individuals are highlighted:

> ITN Asia correspondent J. I. . . . told how he snatched up his five-year-old son Peter and sprinted for safety . . .
> I grabbed him. I could hear the rush behind me and I could see the wall of water coming towards us. When we were about 25 to 50 yards from the beach it caught up with us and it washed us another 50 yards into a mangrove swamp.

These modern disasters are typically described in a 'hygienic' way. Just as doctors are trained not to alarm their patients, so modern journalists describe even the most hideous scenes in a palatable fashion, typically via the 'one little shoe' scenario outlined above. This is unlike early reporting. When, in 1896, the Hon. C. S. Rolls became the first Englishman to die in a plane crash, his injuries were graphically highlighted: 'The biplane reeled in the air and then pitching forward, crashed to earth . . . Mr. Rolls lay doubled up on the driving-seat with blood upon his lips . . . Mr. Roll's face was ashen grey and a large blue bruise marked his forehead.'[24]

A further modern trend is the emphasis on factivity, the presentation of facts and figures which corroborate the data presented, and emphasize its seriousness. Newspaper reports of the disastrous flooding caused by hurricane Katrina on America's Gulf Coast in August 2005 made sure the readers were given plentiful statistics:

the number confirmed dead passed **100** last night in the area which bore the brunt of the **135mph** storm as it smashed ashore . . . While New Orleans escaped Katrina's fiercest winds, a **200ft-wide** hole was breached during the night in a levee, or earth embankment, protecting the city – most of which is below sea level. The water gushed through putting **80 per cent** of the city under water. In some areas it was **20ft deep** . . . the U.S. military dropped **3,000lb** sandbags from helicopters.[25]

Mega-disasters

The tragedies described above lead to a further question: how do newspapers report unprecedented mega-disasters? If 'it is the business of newspapers to create a sensation' – said by the eighteenth-century journalist Henry Labouchere (chapter 5) – what kind of language do newspapers use when they handle truly sensational happenings? The question can be considered by looking at the language used to describe the so-called 9/11 disaster, when on 11 September 2001 two planes intentionally crashed into New York's World Trade Center, whose twin towers burst into flames and collapsed, resulting in multiple deaths.[26]

The death toll was at first the focus of absurdly pessimistic guesswork, which gradually became more realistic: 6,818 are feared to have died, claimed the Deutsche Presse-Agentur and the *Sunday Times* on

23 September 2001. Over 4,000 fatalities, said Jack Straw on the BBC Radio 4 *Today* programme in January 2002. In the long run, 2,672 death certificates were issued, and a further 158 people remained unaccounted for, according to the *Observer* newspaper, 10 March 2002.

But more interesting, perhaps, than the shifting figures, is the language used to describe the disaster. At first, everyone, both politicians and journalists, flailed around seeking for adequate language to cope with the tragedy: 'Oddly, for all the media coverage . . . the events in New York, Washington and Pennsylvania have not yet found a name. Atrocity, outrage, terrorist attack: nothing quite conveys the enormity of it all, and "apocalypse" is overdoing it a little in the absence of four horsemen. The French vision of "megacatastrophe" comes close.'[27] But eventually, certain characteristics of the language used emerged, especially the vocabulary. To some people's surprise, almost all of the words were well-known. Only one apparent neologism occurred, *deathscape*, presumably formed by analogy with *landscape*: 'Fire escapes were gnarled and twisted. . . . Through this *deathscape*, firemen and medics now worked with crazed zeal.'[28]

Nouns and adjectives predominated in the descriptions. In the reports examined,[29] over forty different nouns relating to shock, horror, death and violence were found:

abomination(-s), anguish, apocalypse, Armageddon, assault, atrocity(-ies), attack(-s), barbarism, calamity, carnage, cataclysm, catastrophe, crime, crisis, cruelty, death, deathscape, destruction, devastation, disaster, evil, fanaticism, hatred, horror, inferno, massacre, murder, nightmare, nihilism, obscenity, onslaught, outrage, rage, savagery, shocks, slaughter, suicide, terror, terrorism, tragedy, violence, war.

These nouns sometimes occurred unqualified, for example:

This was an *obscenity*.   (Ian McEwan)
It was an *apocalypse*.   (unnamed survivor)

More usually, one or more of over thirty adjectives accompanied these and other nouns (such as the unemotive *event*).

This has been an *ungraspable tragedy*.
Who could blame the Americans for demanding some type of recompense . . . for the hitherto *unimaginable crime* that had been committed against them?

The adjectives mostly expressed horror and surprise:

amazing, apocalyptic, appalling, atrocious, barbaric, brutal, cataclysmic, deadly, dehumanizing, demented, devastating, evil, explosive, heinous, horrible, horrific, immense, inexplicable, insane, malignant, monstrous, murderous, searing, shocking, spectacular, terrible, terrorist, traumatic, unbelievable, unconscionable, ungraspable, unimaginable, unprecedented, unspeakable, vast.

These adjectives (qualifiers) were mostly attached to nouns. The following three dozen or so qualifier–noun sequences occurred (in alphabetical order of the qualifiers), some of them as two-word descriptions, others as part of longer sequences:

apocalyptic atrocity, apocalyptic nihilism, appalling attacks, atrocious ingenuity, barbaric terrorism, bloody act, cataclysmic abominations, catastrophic morning, deadly

accomplices, deadly sequence, dehumanizing hatred,
demented sophistication, devastating attack, devastating toll,
evil fanatics, explosive destruction, fanatical assault, frenzied
fanaticism, hate crime, immense catastrophe, insane courage,
kamikaze attacks, kamikaze planes, malignant rage, mass
murder, monstrous calling-card, murderous martyrdom,
murderous violence, searing experience, shocking act,
terrible act, terrible atrocity, terrible thing, terror attacks,
terrorism crisis, terrorist atrocity, terrorist attack, terrorist
tragedy, terrorists' rage, Tuesday's terror, ungraspable
tragedy, unimaginable crime, unspeakable evil, vast horror.

A number of longer descriptions (three or more words)
were found, for example:

appalling homicidal stunt, big terrible event, brutal
indiscriminate mass murder, carnage and sudden death, cult
of murderous martyrdom, day of mass murder, deadly
sequence of hijackings, death on an unbelievable scale, east
coast carnage, evil bloody act that left thousands dead, great
human disaster, hatred-fuelled fanaticism, horrific suicide
attacks, inexplicable assault on freedom and democracy,
largest ever massacre on US soil, most searing experience in
American life in modern times, most spectacular terrorist
attack on the United States, most terrible atrocity the world
has witnessed, orgy of fresh developments, spectacular
terrorist attack, spectacular terrorist exploit, suicide hijacker
attacks on America, terrible thing that has been done to
America, unconscionable suicide attacks, unprecedented and
devastating attacks of September 11th, worst terrorist
atrocity ever on American soil.

Many of the phrases found were polysyllabic. Of the
two-word sequences listed above, over thirty contained
at least one word of three or more syllables. In over ten
of them, both words had three or more syllables:

apocalyptic atrocity (5–4), apocalyptic nihilism (5–3),
atrocious ingenuity (3–5), barbaric terrorism (3–3),

cataclysmic abominations (4–5), demented sophistication (3–5), explosive destruction (3–3), murderous martyrdom (3–3), murderous violence (3–3), terrorist tragedy (3–3), ungraspable tragedy (4–3).

The 'weightiness' of the words used to describe the events of 11 September was noticeable. This reflected the gravity of the event. It illustrates a well-known iconic tendency in language: 'heavy' acts or large numbers tend to be represented by 'heavy' words, the most obvious example being that in almost all languages, plurals are longer than singulars.[30] So an established tendency towards iconicity was exploited, rather than invented.

The words used were mostly well-established ones, as already noted. What characterized them was their variety and accumulation. Figurative language was rare. Metaphor was not a prominent feature, unless 'dead' metaphors such as *nightmare, apocalypse*, were included in the count: such words have by now been applied so frequently to disaster scenarios, that they cannot be regarded as truly metaphorical. An exception was an article by Fergal Keane, who referred to 'the dark corridor of the terrorist mind'.[31] Similes also were sparse: 'We . . . watched the Twin Towers being smashed, like a child's toy',[32] said Orla Guerin, but this was an exceptional description.

Alliteration (adjacent words beginning with similar sounds) was found intermittently:

apocalyptic atrocity, appalling attacks, frenzied fanaticism, murderous martyrdom, synchronized slaughter, terrorist tragedy, the twin-towers tragedy, Tuesday's terror.

Layering, once known as 'bleaching' or 'weakening of meaning', was also rare. These days, the word *disaster* is often used to describe a minor inconvenience: 'The gravy's a disaster: it's got too much fat in it', 'The last wicket fell, . . . so it was another blackwash, another disaster for England'.[33] But the disaster words used in the descriptions of 9/11 were found in their most serious meaning.

Fewer verbs were used to describe the events, though two books were published with titles containing the word *shook*: *The day that shook the world* and *Two hours that shook the world*.[34]

Overall, murders and disasters do not need to be dramatized, they are already dramatic. A glance at any newspaper shows that the more dramatic the story, the fewer literary devices are needed to gild it. So at the most 11 September has reminded people of less-often-used disaster words, such as *apocalypse*, *cataclysm*.

The English language may have been affected in minor ways. The immediate location of the attacks, the cordoned-off area where the towers once stood, was christened 'Ground Zero', reportedly by the rescue services. The term *Ground Zero* dates from 1946, and is 'that part of the ground situated immediately under an exploding bomb, especially a nuclear one'[35] – though the phrase is sometimes used more widely to describe an area devastated by a bomb or other explosion. So this phrase is likely to be more widely used.

Reference to the event itself homed in almost immediately on the date, 11 September:

shocks such as September 11th, the attacks of September 11th, the catastrophe of September 11th, the crisis of September 11th, the crisis that burst on the world on September 11th, the events of September 11th, the September 11th atrocities, the September 11th attacks, the synchronized slaughter of September 11th.

The description of major catastrophic events by the date may become more likely. This is not unknown – references are found to, for example, 'The Bloody Friday atrocity of 21st July 1972', though traumatic events are mostly described by the year, as with the '1914–18 war'.

Overall, the events of 11 September are unlikely to have a major effect on the English language.

The overwhelming final feeling of many is that words are unable to do justice to the emotions aroused by the events. As the nineteenth-century writer Samuel Butler once wrote: 'We want words to do more than they can . . . we expect them to help us to grip and dissect that which in ultimate essence is ungrippable as shadow. Nevertheless there they are; we have got to live with them.'[36]

This chapter has considered mainly the organization of news reports, and has also discussed the reporting of dramatic events. But arrangement of the material, and the handling of drama, is only part of the story. In addition, the language used has usually been skilfully polished, in ways not always apparent to the casual reader, as will be discussed in the next chapter.

CHAPTER SEVEN

Glimmering words

Boiling down and polishing

> When you've got a thing to say,
> Say it! Don't take half a day . . .
> Life is short – a fleeting vapour –
> Don't you fill the whole blamed paper
> With a tale, which at a pinch,
> Could be covered in an inch!
> Boil her down until she simmers,
> Polish her until she glimmers.
>
> Joel Chandler Harris (1848–1908)[1]

A belief exists among some of the public that journalism is simply a matter of stuffing words together in any old order, as in the following extract from John Preston's novel *Ink*: '"I can't write any more," said Hugh . . . "I can't get words to come out properly" . . . Battersby stared at him. "You can't have writer's block," he said. "You're not a writer. This is journalism. It doesn't matter if a few words are the wrong way round."[2] Or, as a letter to *The Times* newspaper suggested: 'Good prose is the selection of the best words; poetry is the best words in the best order; and journalese is any old words in any old order.[3]

But, contrary to this old popular view, the language of journalism is often highly polished, as expressed in the rhyme quoted at the top of this chapter, by Joel Chandler Harris, who is best known as the author of the Uncle Remus stories but was by profession a journalist. The language of journalism is not only polished, it is first and foremost clear.

This chapter will outline some of the writing guidelines followed by journalists, and will also explore the 'grammar' of headlines. It will then briefly consider to what extent headlines are similar to, or different from, other types of polished, compact phrases, as in the language of advertising.

Clear writing

'One needs rules that one can rely on when instinct fails', George Orwell pointed out.[4] Orwell, author of 1984, was deeply concerned with 'language as an instrument for expressing and not for concealing or preventing thought'.[5] Even today, trainee journalists are sometimes taught his precepts of clear writing, more than half a century after the advice was given. 'I think the following rules will cover most cases', he suggested:

1 Never use a metaphor, simile or other figure of speech which you are used to seeing in print.
2 Never use a long word where a short one will do.

3 If it is possible to cut out a word, always cut it out.
4 Never use the passive where you can use the active.
5 Never use a foreign phrase, a scientific word or a jargon word if you can think of an everyday English equivalent.
6 Break any of these rules sooner than say anything outright barbarous.[6]

A number of other 'dos' and 'don'ts' have crept into advice commonly given to journalists. The precepts tie in well with Orwell's suggestions, for example DO start sentences with nouns, DO use simple verbs, DON'T use long sentences, DON'T use abstract phrases, DON'T use many adjectives.

Some of these 'commands' are simple common-sense. Adjectives which can be used are those which cover simple descriptions, such as 'The defendant wore a brown jacket, and white shoes, and drove a silver-coloured car.' Words which are avoided are those which express value judgements, especially if a court-case is involved. These tend to occur only after a trial, not during it: 'This wicked man was sentenced to ten years in jail' might be written after a verdict of guilty had been returned, but the emotive adjective *wicked* is avoided while a trial is in progress.

Almost all advice to journalists boils down to exhortations to express their reports in as straight-forward a way as possible, which is not as easy as it sounds: 'To write simply is as difficult as to be good' is a saying attributed to the novelist Somerset Maugham.[7] The difference between bad and good journalistic writing can be illustrated by a rhyme about a donkey, suggested Harold Evans,[8] who edited the English *Sunday Times* throughout the 1970s:

Bad style:
If I had an ass that refused to proceed,
Do you suppose that I should castigate him?
No indeed.
I should present him with some cereals and observe proceed,
Continue, Edward.

Good style:
If I had a donkey as wouldn't go,
Do you think I'd wallop him? Oh no.
I'd give him some corn and cry out 'Whoa,
Gee up, Neddy.'

In a tabloid in particular, space is limited. Readers require brevity and clarity. Brian Hitchen, one-time editor of London's *Daily Star*, advised: 'Consider how difficult it would be to think of the words you use everyday, and then find smaller ones.'[9] For example, an old bomb was found in a garden in south London, which forced the evacuation of families living nearby. The chief sub-editor called over the young writer covering the events: 'What does "evacuation" mean?' 'People had to leave their homes.' 'Then that's the way to write it.'[10] The young man claimed that he learned more about subbing in the tabloids than in his whole career.

But putting in short words instead of long ones is only part of the skill required by journalists. They have to learn how to keep their writing lively, and also how to pack in large quantities of information in as compact a way as possible.

Keeping it lively

Rebus . . . read the daily paper. They were straining for new, shocked adjectives now, having exhausted their thesauruses.

The appalling, mad, evil, crimes of The Strangler. This insane, evil, sex-crazed man. (They did not seem to mind that the killer had never sexually assaulted his victims.) Gymslip Maniac![11]

Here, the struggle faced by journalists to engage their readers is described by the fictional Scottish detective Rebus, as he hunts the abductor of three schoolgirls. Yet Rebus seems unaware that journalists have more resources than vocabulary at their disposal.[12] Real-life journalists adopt a variety of strategies to make their columns user-friendly. These vary, depending on the paper and on the decade, but the following have been prominent in recent years: bite-sized chunks, direct quotes, sparing use of punctuation, a time-phrase at the beginning of paragraphs, and use of a pseudo-title to introduce newsworthy figures. These are illustrated in the examples below.

First, journalists tempt their readers with bite-sized gobbets of narrative. Paragraphs are typically short, especially if the story is dramatic. In July 2005, terrorists planted a series of bombs in London, which exploded during the morning rush-hour. Three weeks later, the suspected terrorists were identified and arrested. In an account of this event published by a British tabloid newspaper, each of the first ten paragraphs contained fewer than fifty words.[13]

Second, direct speech adds interest to a story. Short, snappy quotes provide extra vividness, as in the following account by an onlooker at the arrest of the London bomb suspects: 'Kay Major, a mother-of-one whose house overlooks Block K, watched as one of the men emerged, "He had his hands up on his head," she said. "I just saw the side of his face. He had dark hair and dark skin and was quite chubby. He had no top on.'[14]

Third, punctuation is kept simple. Full stops are common. Colons (:) are rare, semi-colons (;) are non-existent. Commas are used sparingly, and are sometimes replaced by dashes, which may direct the reader onwards in a swifter way than commas or brackets: 'Minutes later, CS grenades were shot into the flat. But as officers pointed their weapons at the property from a safe distance – mindful that a bomb could be detonated at any moment – no one emerged.'[15]

Fourth, a common way of starting a paragraph is the use of a phrase expressing time, as in 'Minutes later' in the quotation above, or 'Shortly after 10 a.m.' in the extract below. This helps to establish a time frame in a reader's mind: 'Shortly after 10am, armed officers in body armour, helmets and balaclavas began quietly to flood the narrow balcony walkways and paths between the 350 housing association flats in the Victorian redbrick blocks.'[16]

A fifth, increasingly common feature of modern newspaper writing is the use of compressed noun phrases, phrases containing a noun which pack in information in an economical way: a descriptive quasi-title has become a normal way of referring to a newsworthy figure. Parallel to genuine titles, such as 'President Bush', 'Lord Coe', 'Prince William', pseudo-titles abound, as in 'modern megastar Michael Jackson', 'boxing champ Mike Tyson', 'royal photographer Norman Parkinson', 'veteran actress Shirley MacLaine', 'television cook Nigella Lawson', 'travel expert Nigel Carter', and so on.[17] This both saves space, and dignifies the person being talked about, so making him or her seem newsworthy.

But not only people receive such descriptions. Other compact phrases are found. '**Interest rate hopes** lift the market' is typical.[18] Such structures are a feature of modern newspaper language in general, and appear to be 'a reflection of two major factors: the informational purpose of newspaper prose, coupled with the influence of economy'.[19] Newspapers are therefore behaving in a contradictory fashion. On the one hand, they narrate their stories simply and clearly. On the other hand, they are developing a compact and economical written style of the type sometimes found in headlines, whose structure will be discussed below.

Grabbing attention

Attention grabbing in newspapers is done via the front page, with two main stratagems: headlines and pictures. 'You have to get the front page right',[20] Andrew Marr points out. 'Broadsheet or tabloid, this is how editors tend to be judged every day. It is where your worst mistakes are most publicly on display, and where creative headlines or pictures can make a difference, at the margin, to sales.' In this, recent, tabloid-size newspapers have a harder time than old-style, larger broadsheets: there is mostly room for only one truly eye-catching tabloid story on the front page. The *Sun* headline 'GOTCHA' on Tuesday 4 May 1982 over a picture of the sinking of the Argentinian ship *General Belgrano* was an example of a headline which became

Fig. 7.1. The famous 'GOTCHA' Headline, *Sun*, 4 May 1982.

famous, and was instantly memorable, but which highlighted an event of which a large proportion of Britain was ashamed.

According to an old joke, the ideal headline is:

TEENAGE PRIEST IN SEX-CHANGE MERCY DASH TO PALACE.

This pseudo-headline encapsulates a popular view that headlines are just eye-catching words crammed together to create the maximum shock-horror effect. And the novelist Michael Frayn exploits this view in his novel *The tin men*.[21]

Dr Goldwasser, the fictional Head of the Newspaper Department in Frayn's novel, had invented what he called UHL, 'Unit Headline Language'. He had collected multi-purpose monosyllables used by headline-writers, such as *fear, ban, dash, strike,* and fed them into a computer. Then he let the computer build its own headlines from this store of words. So it might start with:

STRIKE THREAT

Then adding one word at random a day, it could tell a story:

STRIKE THREAT BID
STRIKE THREAT PROBE
STRIKE THREAT PLEA

Or the units could be added cumulatively:

STRIKE THREAT PLEA
STRIKE THREAT PLEA PROBE
STRIKE THREAT PLEA PROBE MOVE
STRIKE THREAT PLEA PROBE MOVE SHOCK

STRIKE THREAT PLEA PROBE MOVE SHOCK HOPE
STRIKE THREAT PLEA PROBE MOVE SHOCK HOPE STORM

Goldwasser's headlines are fiction. Real headlines
are structured with a level of skill of which readers are
usually unaware.[22]

Headlines on the front page sell newspapers, and
headlines on the inside pages influence what people
read. Their effect is potentially long-lasting. 'Headlines
and leads are often the only information read or
memorized', it has been claimed.[23] And they can have
an immediate effect. When a popular British retired
boxer, Frank Bruno, had a mental breakdown, The *Sun*
newspaper's first edition had a headline: BONKERS
BRUNO LOCKED UP. This brought a deluge of complaints. '*The Sun* belatedly realised how badly they
had misjudged the public mood . . . Later editions
sadly announced SAD BRUNO IN MENTAL HOME
and the following day the tabloid launched a mental
health appeal.'[24]

Headlines grab attention via their subject matter,
their style or preferably both: KNIFE NUT KILLS GIRL
headed an account of a stabbing in the *Sun* (1992).
GAZZA HAZZA PIZZA LUVVA, introduced a story about
the soccer player Paul Gascoigne who had reportedly
'found new happiness with a busty pizza waitress'.[25]
CANNIBAL KILLER CAGED FOR LIFE told of a sadistic
killer whom the judge recommended should never be
released.[26] HEADLESS BODY IN TOPLESS BAR is a
famous headline from the *New York Post*.[27] DENISE IS
TOTTY WITH TOP BOTTY headed a British story of a
'TV babe' who had won a 'Rear of the Year' award, and
who claimed that lots of sex 'kept her botty trim'.[28]

Fig. 7.2. Totty with top botty, *Sun*, 22 October 1999.

FLOODY HELL was the huge headline over a warning to the country 'to brace itself for the worst floods in a hundred years'.[29] PERV GRABS TOT ran an emotive headline,[30] yet a glance at the story revealed that the 'perv' was someone who had in the past been accused of paedophilia, but was in this case accompanied by his wife. The couple had tried jointly to take their own child abroad, who was officially in the care of social services.

Headlines are printed in large bold capital letters, which spread across the page. As in telegrams, surplus words such as the articles *a*, *the*, are routinely omitted, as are predictable verbs such as *is*, *has*. Such omissions can cause unintentional humour, as in the well-known ambiguous example GIANT WAVES DOWN QUEEN MARY'S FUNNEL, and DACOITS SHOOT DEAD POLICEMAN in an Indian newspaper. 'Why did dacoits (bandits) bother to shoot a dead policeman?' queried one puzzled reader.

Short words are used to save space:

AXE, not *closure*: SMALL SCHOOLS FACE AXE
BAN, not *prohibition*: NEW BAN ON DEMONSTRATIONS
MOB, not *crowd*: MOBS RAMPAGE THROUGH CITY STREETS
QUIT, not *leave* or *depart*: CHURCH LEADER QUITS
WED, not *marry*: BISHOP TO WED ACTRESS[31]

Puns are prominent: PAIN STOPS PLAY reported the *Sun*, when a cricketer was bitten by an adder. PORK CHOP, also from the *Sun*, announced that pork had been banned from a pub. PANDAMONIUM was a zoo story in the *Los Angeles Times*.[32]

Yet headlines are not inevitably jokey. The greater the tragedy they are highlighting, the more

straightforward the headline, and the larger in size.
After the London terrorist bombings in July 2005, the
headlines were stark.[33] LONDON'S DAY OF TERROR,
said the *Guardian*. BLOODIED BUT UNBOWED announced the *Daily Mirror*. SUICIDE BOMBER ON THE NO
30, proclaimed the *Sun*, with the added strapline
TERRORIST BLOWS BUS TO BITS. *The Times's*
headline simply highlighted the date in large blue
numbers, 7/7, reminding readers of the American
disaster of 9/11 (chapter 6).

Before the end of the month, a huge police
operation ended with the arrest of the main suspects.
The headlines the next day, 30 July, could be read from
yards away: GOT THE BASTARDS! yelled the *Sun*. GOT
THEM shrieked the *Daily Mirror*. SURRENDER! bellowed
the *Daily Mail*. The day after, 31 July, the Sunday papers
continued in the same vein: CORNERED! shouted the
Sunday Times, RUN TO GROUND echoed the *Observer*. In
short, the more dramatic the headline, the fewer the
words and the larger the type-face. And in recent
papers, a massive colour picture is placed alongside
the huge headline.

Changing headlines

Headlines change over the years. Older headlines
tend to cover the same topics as today's, but without
the current streamlined wording:

FRIGHTFUL TRAGEDY IN SOHO
HORRID MURDER AT BARNSLEY
MELANCHOLY SUICIDE OF A CITY SOLICITOR
THE ALLEGED POISONING OF A FAMILY AT BERMONDSEY
THE HORRIBLE MURDER AT EAST ACTON

These occurred in the *News of the World* in 1854,[34] showing features that have been eliminated a century later, such as evaluative adjectives (*frightful, horrid, melancholy*), the articles *a* and *the* and prepositions such as *in, at.* Today's headlines would be more likely to read: SOHO TRAGEDY, BARNSLEY MURDER, CITY SOLICITOR SUICIDE. Some features remain, such as the fact that time is rarely mentioned.

In 1888, headlines relating to Jack the Ripper (chapter 6) looked fairly similar to the earlier *News of the World* headlines, as in the following triple-deck headline:

A REVOLTING MURDER
ANOTHER WOMAN FOUND HORRIBLY MUTILATED IN
    WHITECHAPEL
GHASTLY CRIMES BY A MANIAC[35]

Jack the Ripper was at first known as 'Leather Apron', as in the following deck of 1888 headlines from the *Star*, which shows a structural parallelism to the *News of the World* ones quoted above:

LEATHER APRON.
THE ONLY NAME LINKED WITH THE WHITECHAPEL
    MURDERS.
A NOISELESS MIDNIGHT TERROR.[36]

These Ripper headlines show a trend which escalated, that of a large quantity of headline information. In the 1930s, multi-deck headlines sometimes tried to cover a whole news story:

69 CHILDREN DEAD IN BRITAIN'S WORST CINEMA
    DISASTER.

SUFFOCATED IN STAMPEDE FROM FIRE ALARM.
HUNDREDS TRAMPLED ON IN A PAISLEY HALL.
QUARTER OF A MILE OF WEEPING MOTHERS.
HOSPITALS GUARD AGAINST ANGUISHED PARENTS.
BROTHERS AND SISTERS KILLED.[37]

Modern British headlines, in contrast, try to repeat the start of a story, and often summarize the first paragraph:

FRENCH STUDENT FEARED MURDERED
Detectives searching for Céline Figard, the French student who went missing after accepting a lift from an English lorry driver, fear she may have been murdered.

FATHER'S PLEA AS SEARCH FOR FRENCH GIRL IS STEPPED UP
The father of a French student missing for more than a week made an emotional appeal to the public yesterday to help find his daughter.

CELINE'S BODY FOUND IN LAY-BY
Céline Figard, the missing French student, was found dead yesterday near a lay-by in Worcestershire.[38]

These headlines were from an (electronic) broadsheet, the *Electronic Telegraph*. A similar pattern occurs in tabloids, as in the following account from the *Sun*:

TRAIN SEX MONSTER MURDERED ISABEL
Pretty law student Isabel Peake was murdered by a sex monster who threw her from a French train, detectives feared last night.[39]

Yet modern headlines are complex. Closer inspection shows that they contain hidden patterns, of which most readers are unaware.

Noun sequences

A strong feature of British headlines in recent years has been heaped-up nouns. Noun sequences of the type ALISON MURDER CHARGE are common in newspapers today. They are a British post-1960s pattern,[40] and tend to confuse foreigners, who are unsure whether *Alison* is the victim or the criminal. Yet speakers of British English are in no doubt: Alison is the victim. Headlines have an internal structure which allows habitual newspaper readers to interpret them without difficulty.

Both broadsheets and tabloids follow the same, semi-rigid patterns in noun sequences relating to similar events, though different topics show slightly different configurations. The section below examines the arrangement of nouns surrounding the word *murder*.

These sometimes form the whole headline, as in ALISON MURDER CHARGE, sometimes only a part of it, as in CAR MURDER HUBBY CAGED. The patterns were analysed in a study of headlines which included noun sequences containing the noun *murder* over a six-month period.[41] The study included both broadsheets and tabloids.

Noun sequences containing the word *murder* occurred in two-, three- and four-word groups.

In a two-word group, the noun *murder* could either precede or follow the other noun:

Sex fiend wanted over BARMAID MURDER (*Daily Mirror*)
MURDER TRIAL told of kamikaze threat (*Guardian*)

In a three-word group, the word *murder* usually came second. Typical sequences were:

BRIDE **MURDER** TRIAL
3-GIRL **MURDER** RAP
STREET **MURDER** ENQUIRY
SHOTGUN **MURDER** HORROR

First came the victim (most commonly), such as *Alison*, *bride*, or (sometimes) the murder location (e.g. *street*), or the murder weapon (e.g. *shotgun*). The final word was a legal term (e.g. *trial*), though might also be a general descriptive noun (e.g. *horror*).

Sometimes, though less frequently, three-word sequences began with the word *murder*, in which case the second word was a legal or abstract term, and the third some involved person:

MURDER TRIAL JUDGE praised

Occasional four-word groups were found, and these mostly involved a victim placed in front of the three-word groups described above:

BOY **MURDER** CHARGE MAN in court

The murder headlines therefore showed a clear murder noun-sequence formula:

A Victim (most likely) or place or cause
B Word *murder*
C Legal or abstract term
D Person involved

The two-word sequences were A + B ALISON MURDER or B + C MURDER CHARGE. The three-word sequences were A + B + C ALISON MURDER CHARGE. The occasional four-word sequences were A + B + C + D BOY MURDER CHARGE MAN (Fig. 7.3, p. 136).

Murder formula

	A Victim/Place/Cause	B murder	C Legal/Abstract	D Person involved
2-word	barmaid	murder		
	M50	murder		
		murder	charge	
		murder	fear	
3-word	Shaughnessy	murder	trial	
	street	murder	enquiry	
	Alison	murder	charge	
		murder	charge	man
		murder	trial	mistress
		murder	case	hubby
4-word	boy	murder	charge	man
	Carl	murder	quiz	man

Fig. 7.3. Murder headline formula.

Both broadsheets and tabloids followed this same basic formula. The main difference between newspapers was in the vocabulary. The broadsheets preferred to use surnames, while the tabloids mainly used the first names of victims:

SHAUGNESSY MURDER TRIAL   (*The Times*)
ALISON MURDER CHARGE   (*Sun*)

The broadsheets used relatively formal vocabulary to describe relationships, such as *mother, father, husband, child, friend*:

Jury in CHILD MURDER CASE was misled.   (*Guardian*)

The tabloids, on the other hand, mostly referred to humans via short, informal vocabulary, such as *mum, dad, hubby, tot, pal*:

CAR MURDER HUBBY caged.   (*Sun*)
Tot is silent witness to MUM'S MURDER.   (*Mirror*)

Finally, the broadsheets used fairly formal legal or technical vocabulary, with words such as *charge, inquiry*:

Driver faces triple MURDER CHARGE.   (*The Times*)

The tabloids used mostly informal vocabulary, such as *rap, quiz*:

Husband on MURDER RAP.   (*Mirror*)

The words *death* and *killer*, showed similar, though mildly different patterns, to *murder*. The overall violent death configurations are shown in Fig. 7.4 (p. 138).

Linguistically, these patterns may have a wider significance. They show how pragmatic patterns, in

Violent death headline formulas

Victim	A Cause	Place	B Key-noun	C Legal/Abstract	D Person involved
xx	x	x	murder	xx	x
xx	xx	x	death	xx	x
xx	x	x	killer		x

xx highly probable; x fairly probable

Main patterns

	2-word	3-word	4-word
Murder:	A+B, B+C	A+B+C, B+C+D	A+B+C+D
Death:	A+B, B+C	A+B+C, B+C+D	
Killer:	A+B, B+D		

Fig. 7.4. Violent death headline formula.

this case words arranged in a newsworthy order, can become habits, and habits become near-'rules'. This may shed light on how language evolved among humans at its beginning.[42]

But these newspaper reports show one further, important factor, and this is their rating of 'newsworthiness'. Victims named were most likely to be female. In the reports, there was an imbalance between the sexes, with more female victims than male reported (325 female to 280 male). Yet according to official crime figures published by the Home Office there were more male victims of fatal violence than female (382 male to 240 female).[43] Female victims seem to newspapers to be more newsworthy than male ones.

Other compact phrases

The compressed noun phrases found in headlines and news stories are sometimes similar to those found in marketing catalogues that, possibly in order to save space, have dense descriptions of household items for sale:

SECURITY DOOR CHAIN GUARD
5-PIECE FAMILY SIZE MIRROR POLISH FINISH STAINLESS STEEL TEA SET.[44]

Catalogues with 'new ideas for kitchen and home' provide numerous similar examples:

FOLDAWAY ALUMINIUM PICNIC SET
INSULATED STAINLESS STEEL CAFETIERE
HIDEAWAY HOME OFFICE

DUCK DOWN WRAP-AROUND DUVET
CLIP-ON TALKING PEDOMETER[45]

This dense style is not unlike some of the phrases found in advertisements, as will be outlined below.

The language of advertisements

'The great Art in writing Advertisements, is the finding out a proper Method to catch the Reader's Eye; without which a good Thing may pass over unobserved',[46] Joseph Addison noted in 1710.

Advertisements show many of the same features as newspaper headlines and 'home catalogues': few words, stylized formulae, puns and word play, all designed to catch attention. Yet it is difficult to find a satisfactory definition of 'advertising'. A broad definition might be 'the promotion of goods or services, usually for sale'. Promotion can be done in various ways, via film, pictures, written words, sounds. Only the written sections of English advertisements will be considered here (even though they are only a proportion of the overall material available).[47]

Advertising has links not only with headlines (as already noted), but also with poetic language. Advertising jingles would barely be recognized as 'poetry', yet they incorporate a variety of poetic devices.

Rhymes are widespread, though more as intermittent catch-phrases, than as fully worked poems: 'Beanz meanz Heinz' is a widely appearing ad for baked beans. 'Set it and forget it' says an ad for a ceramic hob with a timer that can be programmed in advance.[48] 'Murray mint, the too good to hurry mint' describes a candy which is sucked. 'A Mars a day helps you work, rest and play' is the easily memorable slogan for a well-known candy bar. 'Tightens, brightens' occurs in an ad for eye cosmetics.

Alliteration (recurring initial sounds) is common, as in 'Make mine Myers' (a beer ad), 'Players please' (an old cigarette ad). 'Kellogg's cornflakes', a breakfast cereal, has a repeated [k] sound. Assonance (repeated vowels, without rhyme) is also found, as in the name of an eye cosmetic 'Eye Revive . . .' with the repeated vowel sound *eye* [ai]. Consonance (repeated final sounds without rhyme) occurs intermittently in phrases such as 'his and hers', and also in the 'Players please' and 'Beanz meanz Heinz' ads already mentioned.

Some prosodic (sound patterning) features are of long standing, such as the rhythmic 'heaviest last' tendency, the 'X and Y and snaggle-toothed Z' or 'Behagel's Law of increasing members' found in early Indo-European times (chapter 2). It pops up in numerous ads:

Mellow, slightly sweet and a little bit nutty . . . Light, versatile, and ideal for cooking . . .   (Jarlsberg, a type of cheese)

Refreshes, tightens, brightens in the blink of an eye
                              ('Eye Revive' eye cosmetic)

Yet none of these intermittent sound effects occur as often as two other devices, which advertisers use to grab attention – repetition on the one hand, and parallelism on the other, as in the following hair-care ad: 'With Nutrasome, your hair will look thicker, feel thicker, be thicker. If you don't have as much hair as you want, you can now make the most of the hair you have thanks to Nutrasome Shampoo and Supplement. Nutrasome is a breakthrough in the treatment of thinning hair' (ad in *Sunday Times* newspaper).[49]

This short ad repeats the words *you* and *hair* four times each, and *Nutrasome* and *thicker* three times each. The parallel phrases 'look thicker, feel thicker, be thicker' are carefully placed between two occurrences of the word *hair*.

Word play is fairly common in modern British advertisements. 'If you're serious about healthy eating, here's your starter . . .' begins an ad for an oven. In real life, puns often cause groans. Yet in ads, they catch attention. 'Shoes designed to move you' claimed an ad for stylish footwear (Fig. 7.5).

'Better in jams than strawberries' said an ad for a small car. 'I must have left it behind' was a well-known ad some years back, picturing a plump man searching for a tin of Andrews' Liver Salts, which is in his back trouser pocket.

Ads are like headlines in that they are designed to catch attention. Linguistically, they are similar in that they often omit 'little words' such as *a* and *the*, they do not necessarily contain verbs, and may include a playful, punning component. Yet in other ways, they are very different from headlines. Unlike headlines, numerous descriptive adjectives are found in ads, such as *mellow, sweet, nutty, light, versatile, ideal*, as in the cheese ad quoted earlier. Ads also try, sometimes desperately, for variety. Their writers try to make them unique, whereas headlines tend to follow predictable

Fig. 7.5. SHOES DESIGNED TO MOVE YOU.

patterns – indeed, they have to if they are to be understood by readers.

This chapter has discussed the clarity and polish used in good journalism. It has also looked at similarities and differences between headlines and the language of advertising, and pointed out that advertisements use a variety of poetic devices. The next chapter will consider poetic language.

CHAPTER EIGHT

Painting with words

Imaginative creativitiy

> The poet's eye, in a fine frenzy rolling,
> Doth glance from heaven to earth, from earth to heaven;
> As imagination bodies forth
> The form of things unknown, the poet's pen
> Turns them to shapes and gives to airy nothing
> A local habitation and a name.
> > William Shakespeare, *A Midsummer night's dream* (1596)[1]

Inspiration rather than perspiration is the essence of poetic creativity, it is sometimes assumed. Shakespeare's assertion (in the quotation at the top of the chapter) that the poet's pen creates shapes out of 'airy nothing' reflects the popular perception of poetic endeavour, as conjuring with language in a state of artistic ecstasy (Fig. 8.1, p. 146).

Only in recent times have poets freely admitted that imaginative writing may be hard work. Poetry must seem effortless, William Butler Yeats pointed out (1904),[2] even though one line might in fact be the result of prolonged labour:

Fig. 8.1. Conjuring with language.

> I said 'a line will take us hours maybe,
> Yet if it does not seem a moment's thought
> Our stitching and unstitching has been naught.'

And Seamus Heaney in his poem 'Digging' refers to his pen as a spade.[3] He is, he suggests, following in the footsteps of his father and grandfather who used spades as physical tools:

> Between my finger and my thumb
> The squat pen rests
> I'll dig with it.

Poets work at polishing their words, much like the journalists and advertisers discussed in the last chapter. This chapter and the next will outline how poetic creation might be similar to, or different from, journalists' compositions.

But first, let us consider the output of the 'poet's pen'. What exactly is poetry?

What is poetry?

> Welcome, poetic art,
> Of many forms, many faces, many spells,
> noble, well-linked lady.[4]

These Early Irish lines, written in the seventh century AD, emphasize the range and diversity of poetry. Poetic creation antedated writing by tens of thousands of years, and was for millennia purely oral (chapter 2). It was at first used not only to entertain, but also, and possibly more importantly, as a means of preserving traditional knowledge. Accordingly, views about the purpose, and aims, of poetry have changed enormously over the centuries. Definitions tend to be all-embracing. As a recent writer expressed it: 'Poetry is unlimited in its range of subjects . . . It can use all types of diction and idiom . . . Poetry can be, say or involve anything.'[5]

This raises a basic question: if 'anything goes', as the above quotation suggests, can poetry be defined at all?

The word *poetry* is ultimately derived from the Greek verb *poieo* 'make, create', so a *poem* is essentially 'something created'. But this broad description could as easily apply to a jam-tart. It is difficult to find a more precise definition.

'I could no more define poetry than a terrier can define a rat, but we both recognize the object by the symptoms it provokes in us', the poet A. E. Houseman

stated in the early twentieth century.[6] The writer and
thinker Arthur Koestler said that if a line of poetry
strayed into his memory while shaving his skin brist-
led, he got a shiver down his spine, and he stopped
being able to shave.[7] Let us consider what caused
these strange sensations. Perhaps it is metre and
rhyme, which are typically associated with poetry,
as in Walter de la Mare's poem 'Silver':

> Slowly, silently, now the moon
> Walks the night in her silver shoon;
> This way, and that, she peers, and sees
> Silver fruit upon silver trees.[8]

Poetry's rhythmic 'beat' is ultimately derived, it is
sometimes claimed, from the beating of the human
heart, though the poetic beat, based on the syllable, is
expressed in different ways in different languages.
Classical Greek and Latin had rhythmic metres which
interleaved long and short syllables. English uses
strong versus light syllables.

In English, a basic *dum-dee* rhythm is found in
nursery rhymes:

> Jack and Jill went up the hill
> To fetch a pail of water;
> Jack fell down and broke his crown
> And Jill came tumbling after.[9]

This basic rhythm is also found in numerous hymns:

> Now the day is over
> Night is drawing nigh
> Shadows of the evening
> Steal across the sky.[10]

This *dum-dee* (trochaic) unit of rhythm forms a so-called
'foot'. Yet it is not essentially 'poetic'. Many phrases in

normal conversation contain repeated trochaic feet, as in some standard 'freezes', words which have become welded together in a fixed order. We say:

black and white, cup and saucer, hale and hearty, hot and cold, neat and tidy, rum and raisin, salt and pepper, sick and tired, sweet and sour, wet and dry.

Reversing any of these pairs produces an arhythmic, odd-sounding phrase. It is not 'wrong' to say *cold and hot*, or *saucer and cup*, it just sounds less normal.

Poetic metre is of course often more complex than the basic *dum-dee* heartbeat rhythm outlined above. And other things, apart from the heart, can inspire the rhythm, as in W. H. Auden's 'Night mail', which simulates a chuffing train:

This is the Night Mail crossing the Border,
Bringing the cheque and the postal order.

Letters for the rich, letters for the poor,
The shop at the corner, the girl next door.[11]

Alongside metre often comes rhyme, which (in English) typically links lines together. As the seventeenth-century writer Samuel Butler wrote (1663):

For rhyme the rudder is of verses,
With which like ships they steer their courses.[12]

Yet rhyme is optional:

Ask no rhyme
of a poem, only
that it keep faith
with life's rhythm

advises the Welsh poet R. S. Thomas.[13] The American poet William Carlos Williams wrote poetry that sounds at first hearing like a sensitive person talking prose:

> I am a writer
>   and I take
> great satisfaction
>   in it
>
> I like to time
>   my phrases
> balance them by
>   their sensual
>
> qualities and make
>   those express
> as much as
>   or more
>
> than the merely
>   literal
> version of the thing
>   could ever tell.[14]

Williams's poem is written in 'free verse', a translation of French *vers libre*, meaning verse that does not conform to conventional patterns of rhyme and metre. His lines are more carefully structured than some rhyming verse, where rhymes can seem laughably forced, sometimes intentionally so:

> What's the opposite of actor?
> The answer's very simple: tractor.
> I said that just because it rhymes,
> As lazy poets do at times.[15]

As the examples above show, there is a sliding scale between 'ordinary' language and poetic language, and they sometimes overlap quite substantially. But there is more to poetry than metre and rhyme. Poetic language is multi-stratified, and needs to be considered layer by layer.

Layers of language

'How shall I be a poet?' an enthusiastic young lad asked an elderly sage in one of Lewis Carroll's poems. He received more than fifteen verses of instruction, with such advice as:

> For first you write a sentence,
> And then you chop it small;
> Then mix the bits, and sort them out
> Just as they chance to fall:
> The order of the phrases makes
> No difference at all.[16]

These lines of gibberish are quite unhelpful: it is not true that the order of phrases makes no difference, nor are bits chopped, mixed, and left to fall.

Language structure is a series of interwoven layers: sound patterns (phonology), word formation (morphology) and word arrangement (syntax).[17] Each layer is supported by carefully chosen and skilfully woven words:

SOUND PATTERNS
(PHONOLOGY)

WORD FORMATION
(MORPHOLOGY)

WORD ARRANGEMENT
(SYNTAX)

Let us consider these layers in turn, especially how they relate to poetic patterns.

Innumerable bees and clip-clopping horses

> The moan of doves in immemorial elms,
> And murmuring of innumerable bees.[18]

Alfred Lord Tennyson's lines which mimic cooing
doves and humming bees are a famous example of
onomatopoeia, words whose sounds resemble the
objects or animals with which they are associated.
Onomatopoeia is sometimes considered to be the
essence of poetic language. Yet the topic is a complex
one. Onomatopoeia is a mixture of universal
tendencies and idiosyncratic patterns adopted by
individual languages.

Some onomatopoeia is widespread. All over the
world, birds tend to be named after the sounds they
make.[19] *Cuckoo* is perhaps the most obvious, and
often makes its way into English poetry:

> The cuckoo told his name to all the hills

says Tennyson (1842).[20] Owls also are imitated in
poetry:

> Then nightly sings the staring owl,
>   Tu-who;
> Tu-whit, tu-who – a merry note,

writes Shakespeare in *Love's Labours Lost*.[21]
And occasional other birds are provided with
idiosyncratic trills:

> The lark, that tirra-lirra chants

says Shakespeare in *The winter's tale*.[22]

Yet apart from cuckoo calls, birds' songs are rarely
perceived as similar across languages, even if their
name is onomatopoeic. In one dialect of Ojibwa, an

American-Indian language, the onomatopoeic word
jigjigaaneshiinh is a 'chickadee', an English word which
is itself onomatopoeic.[23]

Mostly, poets avoid direct attempts at reproducing
such sounds: birdsong is not so much imitated, as
described, as when Keats in his 'Ode to a nightingale'
(mentioned in chapter 1) pictured the bird as 'pouring
forth thy soul abroad / In such an ecstasy'.[24]

Wind is another source of sound mimicry.
Everywhere in the world, words for blowing tend to
start with *ph*, imitating the whiffling huff of strongly
exhaled breath, as in English *puff*, ancient Greek *phusa*,
though in literature such imitations are found more in
stories and poems for children: 'I'll huff and I'll puff
and I'll blow your house down', threatens the big bad
wolf in the toddler-directed tale of the three little pigs.
In George McDonald's children's poem 'The wind and
the moon', the wind assumed he could blow out the
moon:

> He blew and he blew, and she thinned to a thread.
>   'One puff
>   More's enough
>   To blow her to snuff!
> One good puff more where the last was bred,
> And glimmer glimmer glum will go the thread.'[25]

General noises for sounds intermittently find their
way into rhymes, again usually for children:

> Ding dong bell, pussy's in the well

runs the well-known English nursery rhyme.[26]

Yet even in apparently obvious mimicry, convention
plays a strong role, and onomatopoeic words may have

taken centuries to develop. For example, a sound word *clatter* dates from the eleventh century, and was joined in the fourteenth century by *batter*, *patter* and *smatter*.

But words such as *clatter*, *patter* do not necessarily occur alone. In English, they are often supported by a similar word with a changed vowel, as in *clitter-clatter*, *pitter-patter*, a phenomenon sometimes called 'rhyming formation'.[27]

> 'Bless us,' cried the Mayor, 'what's that? . . .
> Anything like the sound of a rat
> Makes my heart go *pit-a-pat*'.[28]

These lines from Robert Browning's narrative tale *The Pied Piper of Hamelin*, written in the mid nineteenth century, show a long-established front vowel plus further-back vowel pattern: *tiddle-taddle* and *pibble-pabble* are found in Shakespeare.[29] Other well-established examples are the *clip-clop* of horses' hooves, the *ding-dong* of a bell, the *drip-drop* of rain, the *tick-tock* of a clock, and so on.

Yet, in general, 'established onomatopoeia is not notably more evocative than skilful use of descriptive language', as Raymond Chapman points out.[30] Here, as elsewhere, poets are innovative. Even if sound mimicry is used, it is not necessarily conventional. The poet Alfred Noyes (1890–1959) uses *tlot-tlot* rather than the more mundane *clip-clop* to simulate horses' hooves:

> *Tlot-tlot, tlot-tlot*! Had they heard it? The horse-hoofs ringing clear –
> *Tlot-tlot, tlot-tlot*, in the distance? Were they deaf that they did not hear?
> Down the ribbon of moonlight, over the brow of the hill,

> The highwayman came riding,
>   Riding, riding! . . .
> *Tlot-tlot*, in the frosty silence! *Tlot-tlot* in the echoing night![31]

In her poem 'Weather,' Eve Merriam uses an imaginative mix of onomatopoeia and invention to conjure up raindrops:

> Dot a dot dot dot a dot dot
> Spotting the windowpane.
>
> Spack a spack speck flick a flack fleck
> Freckling the windowpane.
>
> A spackle a spatter a wet cat a clatter
> A splatter a rumble outside.
>
> Umbrella umbrella umbrella umbrella
> Bumbershoot barrel of rain.[32]

As these examples show, avoidance of the obvious and imaginative creativity are strong poetic traits.

Good poets not only have a keen ear for sounds, they are also endlessly inventive. One might assume therefore that they would make up their own words. Yet this is rare in serious poetry. Non-words usually identify a work as humorous, as in Edward Lear's poem 'The cummerbund':

> Below her home the river rolled
> With soft **meloobious** sound
> Where golden-finned **chuprassies** swam,
> In myriads circling round.[33]

The nonsense word *meloobious*, perhaps a blend of 'melodious' and 'lubricious', seems at first sight an evocative description of a gliding river, and *chuprassies* might seem a plausible name for a species of fish.

Yet *chuprassies* are in fact a type of minor Indian
official. The poem is immediately marked as
non-serious.

  Non-words, or strange words, are acceptable in
serious poetry in two circumstances. First, when they
are perceived as proper names, as in Samuel Taylor
Coleridge's 'Kubla Khan' (1816):

> In Xanadu did Kubla Khan
> A stately pleasure-dome decree:
> Where Alph, the sacred river, ran
> Through caverns measureless to man
> Down to a sunless sea.[34]

Kubla Khan is not in fact invented, nor is Xanadu.
Kublai Khan was a thirteenth-century Mongol emperor,
grandson of the famous Ghengis Khan. He extended
the Mongol empire to include China, where he had his
summer residence at Shang-du, referred to by
Coleridge as Xanadu, though readers are unlikely to be
aware of this information.

  A second circumstance is when strange words are
presumed to be from a non-standard dialect, as in Tom
Paulin's translation of 'Le crapaud' ('the toad')[35] where
dialect words are used sparingly, enough perhaps to
capture a feeling of strangeness and disgust, but not
enough to turn it into a comic poem:

> An airless night a sort of song
> – moon a metal plaque
> its **tattery** shadows inky green
> . . . buried alive under those laurel roots
> the song's a slimy echo pulsing pulsing
> – he shuts up – look he's down by the drain
> – a toad! his **pursy** skin **pubbles** . . .

To summarize, serious poets do not in general make up words. They exploit existing words, rather than invent new ones. Similarly, when it comes to syntax, minor tweaking only is the norm.

Minor tweaking

> O wild West Wind, thou breath of Autumn's being,
> Thou, from whose unseen presence **the leaves dead**
> Are driven, like **ghosts from an enchanter fleeing**,
> Yellow, and black, and pale, and hectic red.

In these lines, from Shelley's 'Ode to the west wind' (1820),[36] 'leaves dead' rather than 'dead leaves' allows *dead* to rhyme with *red*. And 'ghosts from an enchanter fleeing' rather than the more usual 'ghosts fleeing from an enchanter' was presumably to allow *fleeing* to rhyme with *being*. These modifications show that syntax (word order) is rarely altered too much. Nouns and adjectives occasionally swap places, though not in a way that would lead to a loss of understanding.

The same is true of morphology (word endings and word formation), where only minor tweaking occurs, as when *shoon* replaces 'shoes' (p. 148) so that it can rhyme with *moon*. In John Agard's poem 'The wanted man',[37] the West Indian speaker claims to be mashing up the language, yet the most noticeable alterations are easily comprehensible minor ones, mainly the use of double negatives (*ent* is 'ain't'):

> I ent have no gun
> I ent have no knife
> but mugging de Queen's English
> is the story of my life

I don't need no axe
to split up yu syntax
I don't need no hammer
to mash up yu grammar.

Far more usual than syntactic change is sensitive and
imaginative word usage, as will be discussed below.

A bird with new feathers

Vocabulary sing for me
in your cage of time . . .

You are dust, then a bird
With new feathers, but always
beating at the mind's bars.
A new Noah, I dispatch

You to light awhile
on steel branches, then call
you home, looking for the metallic
gleam of a new poem in your bill.

All poets love choosing and arranging words: this
seems to be basic. And they use them in inventive and
intriguing ways, as R. S. Thomas's lines (above) from his
poem 'Vocabulary'[38] show. Thomas was presumably
working on a typewriter, with his talk of 'steel
branches' and 'metallic gleam'.

Innovative word use is of key importance in
poetry. 'Poets . . . are literal-minded men who will
squeeze a word till it hurts', as the American poet
Archibald MacLeish[39] (1892–1982) expressed it. Or, as a
literary critic somewhat pompously explained: 'Poetry
draws words and their meanings into concentrated
spheres where their expected distinctions and

The child	sleeps
kid	dozes
youngster	nods
tot	naps

Fig. 8.2. Selection and combination.

relationships will be variously unsettled, complicated or re-examined.[40]

Selection from a set of options on the one hand, and **combination** of the forms selected on the other, are the two basic linguistic patterns. This is true of both everyday language, and poetry. As the famous linguist Roman Jakobson expressed it:

> What is the indispensable feature inherent in any piece of poetry? . . . we must recall the two basic modes of arrangement used in verbal behaviour, selection and combination. If 'child' is the topic . . . the speaker selects among . . . more or less similar nouns like *child*, *kid*, *youngster*, *tot* . . . and then . . . he may select one of the semantically cognate verbs – *sleeps*, *dozes*, *nods*, *naps*. Both chosen words combine in the speech chain.[41]

Selection and combination mesh together – in Jakobson's words: 'The selection is produced on the basis of equivalence, similarity and dissimilarity, synonymy and antonymy, while the combination, the build-up of the sequence, is based on contiguity.'[42] Let us discuss this interwoven mesh further.

Like with like

Selection of similar words is one way in which the words of a poem can be welded together. Sometimes, the similarity is absolute – in other words, repetition, as in John Masefield's poem 'The west wind':

> It's a warm wind, the **west wind**, full of birds' cries;
> I never hear the **west wind**, but tears are in my eyes.
> For it comes from the **west** lands, the old brown hills,
> And April's in the **west wind**, and daffodils.[43]

Repetition by itself is not necessarily poetic. It is common in mundane, spoken conversation: "'If I don't prepare and **eat** well, I **eat** a lot . . . So if I'm just **eating** like cheese and crackers, I'll just STUFF myself on cheese and crackers.'"[44] Repetition is even commoner in political speeches. Martin Luther King's famous 'I have a dream' address in 1963 is known by its recurring phrase 'I have a dream', which is repeated more than half a dozen times:

> I say to you today, my friends, . . . **I still have a dream**. It is **a dream** deeply rooted in the American **dream**. I have **a dream** that one day this nation will rise up and live out the true meaning of its creed: "We hold these truths to be self-evident that all men are created equal." **I have a dream** that one day . . .[45]

And George W. Bush reportedly made twenty-seven mentions of the word *freedom* when he was sworn in for his second term as American president.

Repetition is so common in poetry, in political speeches, and in ordinary conversation that there are over twenty different words for it in its various guises, and there may be more:

Alliteration, anadiplosis, antimetabole, assonance, battology, chiming, cohesion, copying, doubling, echolalia, epizeuxis, gemination, imitation, iteration, parallelism, parroting,

perseveration, ploce, polyptoton, reduplication,
reinforcement, reiteration, rhyme, ritual, shadowing,
stammering, stuttering.[46]

Yet straight repetition is used sparingly in poetry. Far
commoner is synonymy, use of words and phrases with
the same or similar meaning, as in the first lines of
John Keats's 'Hyperion' (1820) where he heaps up
different descriptions of absolute silence:

> Deep in the shady sadness of a vale
> Far sunken from the holy breath of morn,
> Far from the fiery noon, and eve's one star,
> Sat gray-hair'd Saturn, **quiet as a stone,**
> **Still as the silence** round about his lair;
> Forest on forest hung about his head
> Like cloud on cloud. **No stir of air was there,**
> Not so much life as on a summer's day
> Robs not one light seed from the feather'd grass,
> But **where the dead leaf fell, there did it rest.**[47]

Opposites

Opposites also play a role. These are more
complex, because several different types exist.[48]
So-called graded antonyms are perhaps the best known,
the term for pairs such as *hot* and *cold*, *deep* and *shallow*,
fast and *slow*. *Hot* and *cold* is a 'graded antonym', in that
no absolute hot or cold exists, but only hot and cold in
comparison to some norm: a hot day means a day that
is hot compared to a normal day's temperature, and
this would undoubtedly be cooler than a hot oven.

Ted Hughes makes use of *cold* versus *hot* in his poem
'The thought-fox' (1957)[49] which describes the creative

process. *Cold* represents his initial slow-moving thoughts. As he struggles to write 'on this blank page where my fingers move', he imagines a fox creeping up:

> **Cold**, delicately as the dark snow
> A fox's nose touches twig, leaf;
> Two eyes serve a movement, that now
> And again now, and now, and now
> Sets neat prints into the snow . . .

The fox gets bolder:

> Till suddenly with a sudden sharp **hot** stink of fox
> It enters the dark hole of the head.
> The window is starless still; the clock ticks
> The page is printed.

Synonyms (same- or similar-meaning words) are not necessarily separated from antonyms (opposite-meaning words). In another poem, 'Witches',[50] Hughes shows his own and possibly other people's ambivalence towards women with a mixture of synonyms and opposites: the words *woman, witch, rosebud, bitch* are interleaved:

> Once every **woman** the **witch**
> To ride a weed the ragwort road;
> Devil to do whatever she would:
> Each **rosebud**, every old **bitch**.
>   . . .
> **Bitches** still sulk, **rosebuds** blow,
> And we are bedevilled.

But synonyms and opposites are not the only lexical relationships.

Missing cover terms

'Blue, green and yellow are colours', 'daffodils,
tulips and crocuses are flowers', 'oaks, beeches and
elms are trees'. Learning these types of groupings are
(or were) typical exercises for schoolchildren. Yet in
real life, cover terms (superordinates) are often hard to
find, and people tend to refer to pairs of items instead:
'Do you have any brothers and sisters?' rather than
'siblings', 'Could you put the knives and forks on the
table?' rather than 'cutlery', and so on.[51] The same is
true of modern poets, who prefer to write vividly
about individual examples, rather than about vague
miscellaneous groups. Ted Hughes's poem 'Thrushes'[52]
specifically refers to this one type of bird:

> Terrifying are the attent sleek thrushes on the lawn,
> More coiled steel than living – a poised
> Dark deadly eye, those delicate legs
> Triggered to stirrings beyond sense – with a start, a bounce,
>   a stab
> Overtake the instant and drag out some writhing thing.

Nowhere in this poem does Hughes mention the word
bird. Nor are such cover terms easily found in the work
of modern poets. An exception comes in Thom Gunn's
poem 'The produce district',[53] when a mindless oaf is
armed with an airgun. The shooting dullard does not
distinguish between different types of bird:

> He stood unmoving on the littered ground
> In bright scrubbed denims
> An airgun loosely in his hands
> Staring at something overhead.

Shooting at birds, he said . . .
He aimed at a parapet some forty-five yards off.
A bang. One pigeon as the others rose
A lump of fluff
Dropped from among them lightly to the street.

Vocabulary in poetry is therefore a matter of precision. But it can also be innovative, particularly in the case of metaphor.

The next chapter will contrast and compare the use of metaphor in everyday speech and writing, in newspapers, and in poetry.

CHAPTER NINE

Two ideas for one

Exploring metaphor

Television aerials, Chinese characters
In the lower sky, wave gently in the smoke.
                                    Douglas Dunn
                    'On roofs of Terry Street' (1986)[1]

Metaphor is possibly the best-known and most
widespread 'trope', an old technical term for figures of
speech which involve meaning. Metaphors are found in
all types of writing, and are held in high regard: 'As to
metaphorical expression, that is a great excellence in
style, when it is used with propriety, for it gives you
two ideas for one; conveys the meaning more luminou-
sly, and generally with a perception of delight.' This
statement was written more than two centuries ago
by the lexicographer Samuel Johnson (1777).[2]

According to the Greek philosopher Aristotle,
metaphor is 'the application to one thing of a name
belonging to another'.[3] To take a modern example,
'Hollywood money isn't money. It's congealed snow,
melts in your hand',[4] said the wit Dorothy Parker. The

topic of the metaphor, here Hollywood money, is usually referred to as the 'target domain', and the new label, here congealed snow, as the 'source domain'.[5] The shared element is known as 'the ground', in this case, presumably the readiness with which both snow and money disappear. Or, in the quotation at the top of the chapter, the television aerials are the target, Chinese characters are the source, and the ground is their shared shape.

Yet Aristotle's definition of metaphor as the misapplication of a name is unsatisfactory, mainly because metaphors which substitute one word for another are not very common. More often, metaphors involve interaction between whole domains, where it is impossible to pick out one single word as substituting for another, as in the following lines from a nineteenth-century hymn:

> Throw out the life-line across the dark wave.
> There is a brother whom someone should save,
> Throw out the life-line, throw out the life-line,
> Someone is sinking today.[6]

Here, a drowning person is being thrown a rescue-rope in a stormy sea. A whole dramatic scenario is involved, and no single word can be pinpointed as the 'metaphor'. Two domains are interacting, not two single words. The same is true of numerous literary metaphors, as when Shakespeare talks of 'nature's fragile vessel . . . in life's uncertain voyage'.[7]

Several questions spring to mind. First, where do metaphors come from? Second, how do metaphors 'work'? Third, why do people use metaphors?

The pervasiveness of metaphor

At one time, metaphor was thought of as literary
and deviant. Yet in recent years, this viewpoint has
been reversed. Metaphor is now recognized as normal
and inescapable. 'Metaphor is pervasive in everyday
life . . . Our ordinary conceptual system . . . is fundamentally metaphorical in nature',[8] as George Lakoff
and Mark Johnson, two pioneers in this area,
pointed out.

Many metaphors are so 'ordinary', that they are
hardly noticed to be figurative. Communication of all
types is routinely described by a 'conduit metaphor',[9]
the idea that a message is packaged up and sent
along a pipe or conduit from one person to
another, as in:

Pauline **put herself across** well.
Peter **got his idea over** at last.
Helen's reasons **came through** clearly.
Alan's words **carried** little meaning.

Similarly, the notion that 'Life is a container'[10] is
ubiquitous:

Geraldine's had a **full life**.
Life is **empty** for Henry.
Alison's **life is crammed** with activity.

Another common metaphor is the idea that 'argument
is war':[11]

Basil's claims are **indefensible**.
Belinda **shot down** Donald's argument.
Stephen **attacked** Mary's viewpoint.

And multiple others can be found in newspapers, books and daily conversation.

The source of metaphors

If metaphors are so all-pervasive, where do metaphorical ideas come from? The answer turns out to be a mixture of long-term ways of thinking, and short-term fashion.

Some ways of thinking may come naturally to the human mind. Humans are unlikely to have pre-printed information in their heads, but, once born into the world, they organize knowledge more easily in some ways than in others. For example, a 'verticality' (up–down) schema is widespread, possibly universal:[12] *up* tends to be thought of as good, and *down* as bad. In English, you can 'go up in the world', or be 'down in the dumps', and this up–down schema is found in other vocabulary items also: '*high* quality' versus '*low* quality', '*on top* of the situation' versus '*bottom* of the heap', '*upper* class' versus '*lower* class'; '*ascend* into heaven' versus '*descend* into hell'. This schema is probably based on experience, though it is not inevitable, and numerous exceptions can be found: a high temperature is bad, so is high blood pressure, and so are rising prices. 'Prime country house prices are rocketing' was the first sentence in an article about finance[13] – though the financial pages equally have articles about falling prices: 'Gold price sinks . . . Bullion prices tumbled to another low yesterday.'[14]

Body metaphors have probably always been a major resource for expanding our word stock, from the origin of language onwards.[15] Humans still extend language in the same way nowadays. In English, we talk about the **head** of an organization, the **mouth** of a harbour, the **foot** of a mountain, the **ribs** of a ship, often without realizing that, strictly speaking, we are talking metaphorically. As well as moving outwards from the body, humans also move inwards: mental activities are expressed in terms of actions of the outer body, as with 'I **see** what you mean', 'Did you **grasp** what he meant?', '**Hold on** to your beliefs.' Even today, the human body is consistently the most frequent source of metaphor, according to one study which analysed figurative language across three centuries[16] – though many of these metaphors are so widespread that speakers may not regard the usages as metaphorical.

In addition to the human body, other world-wide metaphors occur, yet again probably based on human experience, such as the idea that life is a journey. This is found in numerous everyday metaphors, such as:

Belinda *got off to a good start* in life.
Paul's *not getting anywhere*.
Anastasia seems to have *lost her way*.
Herbert's *plodding on*.[17]

Emotions are typically described via metaphors. In the western world, anger is perceived as heated fluid in a container, as George Lakoff has pointed out:[18] anger heats up and swells, the liquid reaches boiling point, and the container finally explodes:

Felicity's anger welled up inside her.
Henry was filled with anger.
Pamela was brimming with rage.

Derek made my blood boil.
Peter had reached boiling point.
Angela's bursting with anger.
Paul couldn't contain his rage.
Felicity just blew up.
John exploded.

In English, just as anger is heat, so fear seems to be the opposite, freezing cold, judging from its metaphors:[19]

Alan's limbs turned icy cold.
Petronella was cold with fright.
Mark was rigid with fear.
Fear froze Angela to the ground.
David was rooted to the spot.

This may be a subconscious attempt to make metaphors tie in with one another, since two alternative courses of action are available to normal humans when they are seriously frightened: they can either freeze, as in English, or flee. Fleeing images are selected in ancient Greek, for example, where even the word for 'fear' is related to a verb meaning 'flee in terror'.

Sometimes, metaphors are relatively short-lived. Typically, currently dominant technology tends to spawn numerous metaphors, which then may fade. In the eighteenth century, clocks and watches were high-tech devices, and so recurred in figurative language: 'The human body is a watch, a large watch, constructed with such skill and ingenuity, that if the wheel which makes the seconds happens to stop, the minute wheel turns and keeps on going round.'[20] These days, numerous metaphors are about computers, with references to hardware, software, input, output, being hardwired, and so on: 'Humankind is as hardwired for curiosity about the future as nostalgia for the past',[21] a Sunday newspaper pointed out. 'Hardwiring memories into your brain'[22] ran the cover 'blurb' for a magazine article about long-term memory.

So far, then, two major points have emerged. First, metaphors are ubiquitous. Second, some metaphors are widespread, and recur across different cultures, while others are short-lived and temporary. But how do metaphors work? This will be considered below.

Prototype theory

Ideas on metaphor are intertwined with theories of word meaning. These underwent a radical change in the mid-1970s. Before then, lexicologists (those who work on the mental wordstore or lexicon) had tried to provide words with fixed meanings, much like dictionaries, where a *mare*, say, might be described as a 'female equine animal'.[23] Such dictionary entries helped to maintain the idea that neat, analytic meanings were the norm, and that metaphors were poetic and peculiar. But then came the change.

In the mid-1970s, an American psychologist, Eleanor Rosch, put forward a new idea, prototype theory.[24] Humans think about word meaning in terms of a super-typical or 'prototypical' instance, she suggested. When they contemplate a bird, for example, they imagine a prototypical one, in America a robin. (American robins are somewhat larger than English ones, though they still have reddish breasts.) People

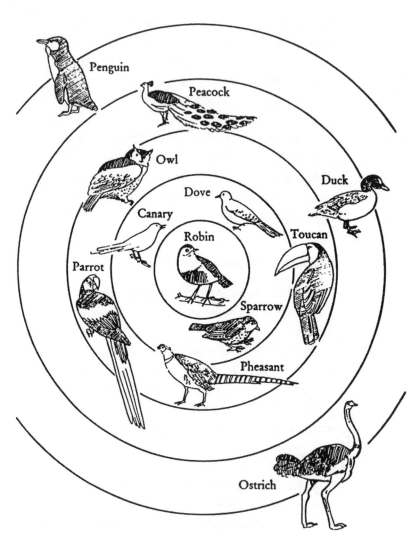

Fig. 9.1. Birdiness rankings.

in Britain usually regard a blackbird as their 'birdiest' bird. Speakers are then able to rank other birds in terms of 'birdiness', with surprising agreement. A canary or a dove is regarded as less good than a robin, though still a reasonable bird exemplar. Toucans, parrots and owls are thought of as not very good, ducks and peacocks are thought of as bad birds, and penguins and ostriches as very bad birds indeed.

Various other categories, such as fruits, furniture and tools also produced surprisingly similar judgements from different speakers, though inevitably differences between nationalities were found, and also differences between age-groups.[25] Fierce arguments arose as to what underlay such judgements.[26] In most cases, they reflect speakers' attempts to make sense of everything around by building up coherent mental models of the world they live in, it was concluded. And metaphor gets fitted into this scheme.

Prototype theory turned out to be important for an understanding of metaphor. No hard dividing-line exists between a word's 'core' meaning, and its outer layers. A metaphor is simply an exemplar that is a long way from the prototype, much as a penguin is a 'funny' kind of bird, though still a bird. Take the word *toboggan*, originally an Algonquian (American Indian) word that was borrowed into Canadian French. At its core, this involves use of a toboggan (a type of sledge), for fast travel downhill over ice or snow.

Yet it is often used in non-core ways. The toboggan may be absent: 'Percy fell over backwards, and tobogganed down the slope so fast, even the ski instructor couldn't catch him.' Even ice and snow are

unnecessary, according to an example in the OED: 'The children got three tin baths and began to toboggan down the grassy slopes in them.'[27] Fast downward travel may be the only essential, as in: 'The whiskey tobogganed down Toby's throat.' As the metaphor examples given so far show, there may be different reasons for using metaphor. These will be considered below.

A magical coat

'The metaphor is . . . a kind of magical coat, by which the same idea assumes a thousand different appearances',[28] said Oliver Goldsmith in the eighteenth century. Metaphor is a magical coat partly because it is so varied, partly because it can be used for a variety of purposes. Ordinary language users, journalists and poets all use metaphors extensively, and for different reasons.

Their most obvious use is to grab attention, as with this description by A. A. Gill, a Sunday newspaper journalist, who suggests that fresh, well-written news is as delicious and nourishing as a good breakfast: 'It has always been this column's policy to pick the juiciest, crispest, most moist and succulent news for your breakfast table. We harvest it in the dewy peak of condition. We endeavour hygienically to offer you news bursting with juicy adjectives and hearty explanation, still steaming from that fresh-from-the-oven yumminess.'[29] Another attention-grabbing description was by the Sunday newspaper journalist, Cosmo Landesmann, who described a lost love: 'She walked

into my life, mugged my heart, coshed my mind with
her wit . . . Ten years later . . . she packed her bags
and left, dumping that happy heart of mine into the
dustbin of her history. Boo-hoo.'[30] But there is a huge
difference between the various sections of a newspaper.
On the news pages, metaphors are rare. Disasters and
murders are often lead stories. They have plenty of
intrinsic drama. They do not therefore need pepping
up with figures of speech. So metaphors are hard to
find if the news is dramatic. Hardly any metaphors
were found in the accounts of the World Trade
Center destruction in the USA in 2001 (chapter 6),
or the descriptions of the Asian tsunami in 2005.

   Another major use of metaphor is to liven up dull
reports. The finance and sports sections of newspapers
are the most in need of being livened up. The metaphors are typically quite simple, and are fully explained
by the writer, especially in the case of finance, about
which many readers are relatively ill-informed:

The **hurricane** tearing through the Asian Pacific economies
is sending a **chill** into the boardrooms of the world's arms
manufacturers.[31]

The economic **meltdown** has **punctured** share prices and
sent currencies **falling**.[32]

Meanwhile, sports writers do their best to liven up
games that are essentially repetitive, such as cricket:

Inspirational Thorpe **digs deep** for England before a bowling
blitz sends Jamaican batsmen **reeling**.
Dean Headley and Andy Caddick **launched** England's winter
campaign with a **bang** as they shared seven wickets in a
storming assault on Jamaica's batting.[33]

Politics also often needs livening up. Robert Harris, writing in the *Sunday Times*,[34] likened his role as a political columnist to an air-accident investigator, someone whose job it is to sift through the wreckage of an aircraft, and to discover what caused the catastrophe. As (in 1996) he looked at John Major's collapsing government, he comments:

It is a vision of absolute chaos. Baggage, seats, wheels, bits of fuselage, miniature bottles from the drinks trolley – all lie strewn and smashed across the landscape. Here, smouldering in a crater, is one wing of the Tory party. There, hanging in the trees, is a section of the other. What has happened is clear enough: a great political machine has simply plunged into the earth.

After considering why this might have happened, he concludes: 'And so one day last week – patched up, iced up, out of fuel, and with the pilot back in the economy section trying once again to separate his squabbling passengers – the whole rickety contraption fell out of the sky.'

Going bananas: other reasons for metaphor

But not all metaphors are there to grab attention and liven up dull sections of a newspaper. They occur for a variety of other reasons, some of them practical, others social.

An important reason is explanation, which can lead to new levels of understanding. The heart is a classic case. It was once thought to be a furnace, but as soon as a pump metaphor was applied to it by Sir William Harvey in the seventeenth century, this explanatory metaphor led to an understanding of its main role within the body. Today also, scientists and good journalists try to get across difficult or dull ideas via metaphors, as in an article about the colonizers of vacant living spaces in the animal world: 'Nature's real estate changes hands all the time', we are told, 'A typical example of what economists call a "vacancy chain" is the housing market among hermit crabs.'[35]

Some metaphors recur. Health metaphors are commonly used by politicians, especially in relation to the economy: 'funds were haemorrhaging out of the lira', 'small businesses are the lifeblood of the nation', 'a desperate attempt to resuscitate the ailing tourist industry', 'we had a very sick balance sheet', 'although the Group is no longer on its death-bed, it is still in convalescence'.[36] The impression they presumably hope to give is that they, the politicians, are in charge of the economic recovery of the nation, and are nursing it back to health.

Metaphor is also used for social reasons, such as euphemism. These days, it is politically incorrect to label anyone 'mad', or 'mentally defective', so a whole raft of new euphemisms has emerged, some of them metaphorical, as with *to go bananas* (Fig. 9.2, p. 178).

A phrase with similar meaning, 'two sandwiches short of a picnic' has spawned numerous copycat metaphors, such as 'Harry's two cans short of a sixpack', 'Gina was two clean napkins short of a picnic basket' and 'Peter's two anchovies short of a pizza.' Over ninety were identified by a researcher at the University of Liverpool.[37] And new ones still pop up, as when a group of Canadian psychologists published a paper

Fig. 9.2. My pear tree has gone bananas.

on the children's book character, the toy bear Winnie the Pooh: 'While not a complete fruitcake, Pooh . . . is certainly a few sultanas short of a full loaf',[38] they suggest.

Mental manipulation is a more worrying social reason for using metaphor. Metaphors are 'high-tech' devices for changing people's minds, the linguist Susan Elgin has argued. She used to be annoyed when friends left their television on when she visited them. Then she realized that, for some of them, the ongoing television replaced the flickering hearth of olden-times. This changed her attitude instantly: 'I wouldn't expect them to put out the fire in their fireplace during my visit: why should they turn off their television?'[39]

Metaphor can be used for more worrying types of manipulation, for example to dehumanize. Drug couriers are typically described as 'mules' or 'ants'. This devalues them as people, and makes their death or imprisonment seem less worrying:

They shipped cocaine into the US via mules who would coat their stomachs with cod-liver oil or honey, then swallow the cocaine wrapped in condoms.[40]

Heroin can count on an army of ants each carrying 2–3 kilos.[41]

Hitler dehumanized Jews, by referring to them as 'Jewish bacilli', his presumed assumption being that Jews are not 'real' people, but harmful bacteria. Similarly, Ronald Reagan used a disease metaphor for people from the Soviet Union. He referred to Marxism as a 'virus', and vowed to fight the 'Communist cancer'.

Metaphor can also give a false notion of security. Politicians who promote the acquisition of nuclear weapons typically refer to them as 'nuclear shields' or 'nuclear umbrellas', so masking the danger of such devices by implying that they are essential protective equipment. In the Gulf War in 1991, air strikes on enemies were spoken of as 'precision bombing' which had 'pinpoint accuracy', carefully avoiding mention of the death and destruction inevitably caused by any bombs.

In a similar vein, metaphor is sometimes used to romanticize dangerous explosions, or at least obscure their perils, as when an atomic bomb project is described via phallic imagery: a US military adviser spoke of plans to release '70–80% of our megatonnage in one orgasmic whump'.[42] Another implied that a nuclear blast was a thrilling sexual experience: 'There came shooting out of the top a giant mushroom that increased the size of the pillar . . . The mushroom top was even more alive than the pillar, seething and boiling in a white fury of creamy foam, sizzling upward and then descending earthward, a thousand geysers rolled into one.'[43]

Presupposition is a further metaphorical 'trick', much loved by some advertisers. Their exhortations to 'Be free!' presuppose that women in particular are prisoners until they use a specific advertised product: 'Be free!! Buy our grill-in-a-minute hamburgers!' This implies that women were previously chained to a cooker cooking. 'Be free!! Use X's super-absorbent tampons!' This suggests that women were previously restricted in their movements at times of menstruation. And so on . . .

But new metaphors do not inevitably 'take off': they need to achieve cultural resonance, by reflecting and capturing the general *Zeitgeist*, or 'feeling of the age'. They must also avoid cognitive dissonance, that is, they must fit in with one another. Otherwise they will seem odd.[44]

So far, metaphors have been shown to be highly varied. In newspapers, they often liven up dull copy, and are a useful explanatory tool. In politics, they sometimes conceal the truth. Poetic metaphors may be somewhat different, as will be discussed below.

Poetic magic?

Poetry is often associated with imaginative metaphors. Yet it would be a mistake to assume that all poetic metaphors are fresh and 'good', and that newspaper and political metaphors are dull and 'bad'. Some poetic metaphors are hackneyed and repetitive, as with the recurring notion that 'life is a bubble': 'life is mostly froth and bubble',[45] said the nineteenth-century poet Adam Lindsay Gordon.

Life as a journey recurs in poetry, and some examples are inspirational, others dull. A key ingredient is a traveller, who follows a route, and has a destination. The most famous example may be Macbeth's statement in Shakespeare's play of that name:

> And all our yesterdays have lighted fools
> The way to a dusty death.[46]

And life as a journey is found in the work of numerous other poets:

> Like pilgrims to th'appointed place we tend;
> The world's an inn, and death the journey's end

wrote John Dryden (1631–1700).[47] Emily Dickinson (1830–86) envisaged death as a coachman, who picked her up as she travelled:

> Because I could not stop for Death –
> He kindly stopped for me –
> The Carriage held but just Ourselves –
> And Immortality.[48]

Robert Frost (1875–1963) saw himself as someone who had taken a less usual route through life:

> Two roads diverged in a wood, and I –
> I took the one less traveled by,
> And that has made all the difference.[49]

This 'travelling' image is not restricted to English poets. The Italian Dante (1265–1321) began his 'Divine Comedy' by describing his life as a journey in which he had lost his way:

> Nel mezzo del cammin di nostra vita
> Mi ritrovai per una selva oscura
> Che la diritta via era smarita . . .[50]

'In the middle of the road of my life, I found myself in a dark wood, in which the direct route had been lost . . .'.

The success of the best poetic metaphors may lie in their unexpectedness, and the multiple possibilities which can be cajoled out of readers/hearers.

Lure to the imagination

A good poetic metaphor typically acts as a lure to the imagination. When humans hear or read a word, a 'spreading activation' process takes place, especially if the word is at all ambiguous. Numerous ideas are triggered off.[51] Gifted poets encourage this spreading, so the hearer or reader may actively contemplate multiple meanings, as in the following lines written by Seamus Heaney:

The royal roads were cow paths.
The queen mother hunkered on a stool
and played the harpstrings of milk
into a wooden pail.[52]

When Heaney talks of the person milking the cow
as playing 'the harpstrings of milk', several interpretations are possible. Is he referring to the musical
noise made by the milk plashing into the pail? Or is
he describing the multi-stringed appearance of the
squeezed-out milk? Or is he drawing attention to the
rhythmic hand-movements of the milker? Possibly, all
of these things, and there may be other images and
sensations which occur to someone who continues
to contemplate these lines.

Or consider lines from Philip Larkin's poem 'Coming':

On longer evenings,
Light, chill and yellow,
Bathes the serene
Foreheads of houses.
A thrush sings,
Laurel-surrounded
In the deep bare garden,
Its **fresh-peeled** voice
Astonishing the brickwork.[53]

The notion of houses having 'serene foreheads' bathed
in light conjures up a peaceful, relaxing image. On
hearing of the thrush's 'fresh-peeled voice', a possible
first reaction is that it is like a newly peeled vegetable.
But the meanings of the word *fresh* are complex. The
most obvious meaning of *fresh* is 'new, recent': 'fresh
eggs' are freshly laid, and 'fresh bread' has been

recently baked. But an overlapping meaning of
fresh is 'clean', 'in good condition', as in *fresh air*.
And numerous similar usages come to mind, such
as *fresh-faced*, *fresh sheets*.[54] Again, the reader's mind is
pulled onwards and outwards. Psychologists refer to
this as spreading activation, as already noted. Literary
critics are aware of the mental process involved,
though have more problems describing it. John
Carey has suggested that it could be labelled
'indistinctness'.[55]

Even poets themselves sometimes see extra layers
in their own work. On one occasion in the early 1960s,
T. S. Eliot was discussing interpretations of his poetry
with students at Harvard University. After he had
suggested several possible meanings of some lines, a
student asked him: 'I've got another interpretation.
Did you also mean this?' Eliot replied: 'What a good
idea! Yes, I think I did.'

Good metaphors elicit, first, surprise, then a sense
of appropriateness, a feeling of 'that's right'. The poet
Craig Raine is a master of metaphor. Writing of Greece,
for example, he describes the fluted columns of
ancient ruins as 'columns of corduroy'. He writes that
'Dolphins darn the sea' between Greek islands.[56]
The imagination is lured on and on.

In another poem, set in England, Raine compares
the fading of a love affair with the darkening daylight
on a winter's day:

> Entering the final phase
> I noticed with a shock
> The year was old
> And light got bruised by four o'clock.[57]

The idea of bruised light intertwines with the notion of a dimming relationship to set off a cascade of fresh fantasies.

But not all metaphors are solemn and serious. They can be light-hearted, as when Roger McGough conjures up a winter scene:

> trees have dandruff
> in their hair . . .
> ponds are wearingglasses [stet]
> with lenses three feet deep . . .[58]

And his description of a shy person who drank too much at a party is hilarious:

> And soon the wine has
> Pushed its velvet fingers down your throat . . .
> Like a vacuum cleaner on heat
> You careered hither and thither
> Sucking up the smithereens
> Of half-digested chat.[59]

This chapter has considered metaphor, and found that it encompasses an enormous variety. Both journalistic and poetic metaphors are often clever and original. The main difference is that journalistic metaphors are overwhelmingly clear and easy to comprehend. Poetic metaphors, on the other hand, are often intentionally ambiguous, a lure to the imagination, so that readers can think up multiple interpretations, and never be sure that they had reached the end of all the possibilities.

But it would be a mistake to call one type 'better' than the other. Each serves its own purpose. The language is fortunate to have both types. One might even say, to quote a phrase from the comic character Puff in Richard Sheridan's play *The critic* (1775), that the language has been enriched by both 'with variegated chips of exotic metaphor'.[60]

The next chapter will continue to explore the relationship between literature and journalism.

CHAPTER TEN

The role of journalism

Evaluating the views

> Thou god of our idolatry, the press . . .
> Thou fountain, at which drink the good and wise;
> Thou ever bubbling spring of endless lies;
> Like Eden's dread probationary tree,
> Knowledge of good and evil is from thee.
>> William Cowper 'The progress of error' (1782)

Mostly in our culture, literature is highly praised and journalism censured (chapter 1). Yet this is an oversimplification. In the past, many of our finest writers have overtly enjoyed newspapers, and sometimes proudly written for them.

At the end of the eighteenth century, Charles Lamb reminisced about how he had written 'witty paragraphs' for a morning paper and was delighted to have been pronounced a 'Capital Hand' (chapter 5). In 1801, Samuel Coleridge, best known as author of 'The ancient mariner', expressed his enjoyment at reading 'a smoking new newspaper'.[1] The nineteenth-century novelist Thomas Hardy has been branded a 'copycat' because some of his best-known storylines were taken

Hardy, the copycat of Casterbridge

Rachel Dobson

A PRIVATE notebook belonging to Thomas Hardy has revealed how the novelist copied many of his best-known story lines from local newspapers in his native Dorset.

Hardy was desperate to keep the notebook secret and asked for it to be burnt after his death in 1928, but it was saved by his executors and is now to be published for the first time.

Among the dozens of articles copied down by Hardy in the notebook is one that formed the basis for the coach crash that was central to the plot of Tess of the d'Urbervilles. Another article recounts a "wife sale" similar to the opening scene of The Mayor of Casterbridge. William Greenslade, princi-

Hutton Getty

frequent method used by men to raise money in the period written about by Hardy.

In the opening scene of The Mayor of Casterbridge, Michael Henchard, an unemployed farm labourer, gets drunk at a fair and sells his wife and child to a sailor for five guineas.

Another entry shows how the action for a wrestling scene in the book between Henchard and Donald Farfrae, the main characters, came from an 1829 report of a wrestling match in St Thomas's parish of Exeter.

Hardy scholars claim publishing the book provides an insight into how the author wanted his books to be partly social history rather than just invention.

Michael Millgate, a Hardy biographer and professor of English at Toronto University, said: "Hardy was always hap-

...al English lecturer at the University of the West of England and editor of the notebook — which Hardy called Facts from Newspapers, Histories, Biographies and Other Chronicles — believes that the author was uneasy at the thought of readers knowing that he had taken some of his best ideas from the local press.

"There is an embarrassment that he feels about his reliance upon these sources and this was why he was so secretive and wanted the book destroyed," said Greenslade.

The notebook, which is to be published early next year by Ashgate, is one of several books that were saved by Hardy's executors when he died in 1928 but is the only one that illustrates him copying news reports from local papers.

Others deal with architecture, painting and literary notes. They are held in the Dorset county museum.

Hardy began the 221-page bound notebook in 1883 and also includes some extracts from histories and biographies of the time. The book mainly consists, however, of systematic note-taking from editions of the Dorset County Chronicle from 1826 to 1830, a time of economic downturn and a much more primitive and lawless society than that of the late 1880s when Hardy was writing.

He was trying to build up a picture of the disintegrating rural society in which several of his novels are set, before the more comfortable urban era in the late 19th century.

Hardy would borrow old editions of the paper from his local library and take them back to his house in Dorchester. There he would read the papers and either copy some of the articles himself or detail Emma, his first wife, to write down the desired extracts. Parts of the notebook are in her hand.

In one entry Hardy notes an account of a coach crash from an edition of the Dorset County Chronicle of August 19, 1830, under the heading "shaft of

Secret inspiration: Hardy noted down a report of a wife sale

wagon enters breast of ridden horse". This crash and small details from others provide the basis for the incident in Tess of the d'Urbervilles when Prince, the family horse, is fatally wounded in a crash with a mail coach.

This proves the end of Tess's family's trading business and puts her on the beginning of a road to ruin. The novel was the basis of one of the best-known films of Hardy's work, made in 1980 and starring Nastassja Kinski as Tess.

There is also an account of a wife sale in Stamford, Lincolnshire, copied by Hardy from the October 1, 1829 edition of the Chronicle. Next to it he has written in pencil "Used in the Mayor of Casterbridge". Selling a family was an illegal but pier if he could find factual historical material to work with rather than just making it up. It portrays him as a historian who used stories in the paper as the basis of plot or specific episodes."

Fred Read, retired senior history lecturer at Warwick University and a Hardy expert, believes that he was looking for more than just colourful stories in his note-taking. He points to a more political side of Hardy, as the notebook also contains accounts of election meetings and poll results in Dorchester.

"He takes a historical interest in the destruction of the peasantry and small farmers and the growth of large estates," said Read. "It shows a more radical and political side to him and how he was trying to immerse himself into a much darker age than his own,"

It is thought that Florence, Hardy's second wife who survived him, probably saved the books from destruction.

Hardy scholars are sympathetic to his view that the notebook should be nobody's business but his own. "He didn't see why he should reveal the notebooks with which he had worked, as he wanted people to read the novel, not the raw material," said Millgate.

Fig. 10.1. The copycat of Casterbridge.

from news reports in the local press.[2] Hardy would reportedly borrow old editions of the *Dorset County Chronicle*, then take them back to his house and either copy down details himself, or ask his wife to do so. A variety of colourful scenes were factual in origin, for example a wife-sale by a drunken labourer in the novel *The Mayor of Casterbridge*.

The novelist Charles Dickens (1812–70) was a prolific and talented journalist. He began his writing career as a reporter for the *Morning Herald*, and 'never quite gave up journalism even in the years of his greatest output as a novelist'.[3] His journalism is often as readable as his novels: 'We had been lying here some half an hour. With our backs to the wind, it is true; but the wind being in a determined temper blew straight through us, and would not take the trouble to go round.'[4] These words described a wait on the river in a Thames Police galley. And in his novel *The Pickwick papers* he makes one of his characters, Mr Weller senior, object to poetry, when he gives advice to his son: 'Poetry's unnat'ral, no man ever talked poetry 'cept a beadle on boxin' day . . .; never you let yourself down to talk poetry, my boy'.[5]

The thrill of journalism is most famously captured in a passage in William Thackeray's novel *The history of Pendennis* (1898).[6] The hero Pen and his friend Warrington were walking along the Strand as they talked. They pass by

a newspaper office, which was all lighted up and bright. Reporters were coming out of the place, or rushing up to it in cabs; there were lamps burning in the editors' rooms, and above where the compositors are at work: the windows of the building were in a blaze of gas.

'Look at that, Pen,' Warrington said. 'There she is – the great engine – she never sleeps. She has her ambassadors in every quarter of the world – her couriers upon every road. Her officers march along with armies, and her envoys march into statesmen's cabinets. They are ubiquitous. Yonder journal has an agent at this minute, giving bribes in Madrid; and another inspecting the price of potatoes in Covent Garden. Look! Here comes the Foreign Express galloping in. They will be able to give news to Downing Street tomorrow: funds will rise or fall, fortunes be made or lost . . . Lord B. will get up, and holding the paper in his hand, and seeing the noble Marquis in his place, will make a great speech; and – and Mr. Doolan will be called away from his supper at the Back Kitchen; for he is foreign sub-editor, and sees the mail on the newspaper sheet before he goes to his own.'

In the twentieth century, the novelist and essayist Virginia Woolf (1882–1941) admired newspaper writing, though recognized that its precision and temporary nature made it different from other types of writing:

The newspaper crocus . . . fills precisely the space allotted to it. It radiates a golden glow. It is genial, affable, warm-hearted . . . It is no despicable feat to start a million brains running at nine o'clock in the morning, to give two million eyes something bright and brisk and amusing to look at. But the night comes and those flowers fade . . . the most brilliant of articles when removed from its element is dust and sand and the husks of straw.[7]

But some other writers treat journalism as a slightly shameful addiction: 'My boy, journalism is a brothel you can enter, but never leave' was said to Michael Ignatieff by his father.[8] And a love-hate relationship is revealed in Hilaire Belloc's poem 'The happy journalist' (1910):

I love to walk about at night
　By nasty lanes and corners foul,
All shielded from the unfriendly light
　And independent as the owl.

By dirty gates I love to lurk;
　I often stoop to take a squint
At printers working at their work.
　I muse upon the rot they print.[9]

Yet attitudes towards journalism, whether in favour, or coldly hostile, are expressions of opinion. These need to be carefully assessed. Let us consider the matter further.

Literature versus non-literature

Typically, 'literature' is evaluated as 'good' in our culture, while 'non-literature' tends to be rated as unworthy of serious attention, as already pointed out (chapter 1).

Yet what is 'literature'? This is unclear, and dictionary definitions are often vague. 'Literature: literary production; . . . writings whose value lies in beauty of form or emotional effect'[10] says one best-selling dictionary. No information is given as to who makes the decisions about the 'beauty of form' or the 'emotional effect', or how the evaluation is carried out.

From the late eighteenth century onward, literature was given a special status, as Rob Pope (among others) has pointed out: 'Literature . . . was narrowed and elevated so as to mean: certain kinds of artistic and aesthetic writing which were reckoned to be especially creative and imaginative . . . Conversely, . . . all writing that was reckoned to be factual and historical was also implicitly stigmatised'.[11]

Yet the divide-point between literature and non-literature is ultimately arbitrary, as John Carey explains: '"Literature" . . . is not an objectively ascertainable category to which certain works naturally belong, but rather a term used by institutions and establishments and other culture-controlling groups to dignify those texts to which . . . they wish to attach value'.[12] Carey continues: 'The question worth asking therefore is not whether reportage is literature, but why intellectuals and literary institutions have generally been so keen to deny it that status.' One factor, he suggests, may be resentment of the masses – a desire to be seen as belonging to a select few who have 'good taste', a superior section of society in which '"High" culture is distinguished from the "vulgarity" said to characterize reportage.'

This admiration of high culture appears to be a tradition handed down from centuries earlier, seen when George Puttenham at the end of the sixteenth century poured scorn on 'blind harpers or such like tavern minstrels' who told stories of the old time 'for recreation of the common people at Christmasse diners and brideales, and in tavernes and alehouses, and other places of base resort'[13] (chapter 4). It was further nurtured by the (now known to be mistaken) belief among prominent intellectuals that a mature language was essentially a written one. Samuel Johnson expressed this idea dogmatically in 1755, when he was disappointed to find that speakers of Earse (a variety of Gaelic) in Scotland were illiterate (chapter 2): 'When a language begins to teem with books, it is tending to refinement . . . speech becomes embodied and permanent . . . By degrees one age improves upon another. Exactness is first obtained, and afterwards elegance. But diction, merely vocal, is always in its childhood. As no man leaves his eloquence behind him, the new generations have all to learn.'[14]

But beyond literacy, another factor, the idolization of the imagination, may be even more important, John Carey suggests: 'The disparagement of reportage also reflects a wish to promote the imaginary above the real. Works of imagination are, it is maintained, inherently superior, and have a spiritual value absent from "journalism". The creative artist is in touch with truths higher than the actual, which give him exclusive entry into the soul of man.'[15] Consequently, in the western world, imagination is possibly overrated and facts are undervalued. As an American writer claimed: 'There is only one real difference between the two forms [journalism and novel writing] – and that is the rigidly vested interest in the maintenance of a polar (or strictly polarized) separation of "fiction" and "journalism" by . . . writers who spent most of their working lives learning, practising, and finally insisting on the esthetic validity of that separation.'[16] Such reverence for the imagination is paralleled by a feeling among many that painting is more valuable than photography.

Yet over and above the long tradition that literature is good, and journalism bad, an important further reason for disapproval is possibly ignorance of the journalistic conventions, some of which were discussed in chapters 6 and 7. Every genre has its own habitual patterns, and people often (mistakenly) judge newspapers by literary conventions. Yet newspapers cannot suddenly change their character, any more than the Houses of Parliament could suddenly host pop concerts. Furthermore, the media have an important role to play in the creation and maintenance of shared values and beliefs, as will be explained below.

A thick blanket of fog

Fog Chaos Grips South
A thick blanket of fog lay across southern England this
    morning like a thick blanket –
'Don't let's call it a thick blanket today, Joe, let's call it a
sodden yellow eiderdown.'
'Are you insane?'

This short piece/poem by Adrian Mitchell, entitled 'Early shift on the *Evening Standard* news desk'[17] reflects the intentional conservatism of many newspaper columns.

Newspapers give their readers a comforting sense of security, and continuity. Journalists provide further instalments of the news stories featured on previous days, such as a hunt for a killer, which is treated almost like an ongoing soap opera. Progress in the search for the missing student Céline Figard, for example, was announced in the headlines summarizing the successive days' stories: 'French student feared murdered', 'Father's plea as search for French girl is

stepped up', 'Céline's body found in lay-by'
(chapter 7).

Furthermore, the news stories covered fit in with
the readers' preconceptions about 'normal' newspaper
topics, the murders, plane, train and car crashes which
readers expect. As Andrew Marr notes: 'It is not
uncommon to leaf through four tabloids and four
broadsheets and find almost exactly the same
stories in every one.'[18]

Rudyard Kipling illustrates readers' expectations
with a short story written towards the end of the
nineteenth century, about three journalists on a
voyage from Cape Town to Southampton.[19] Their ship
was almost sunk by an underwater volcano which also
disgorged a huge sea-serpent: 'He had been spewed up,
mangled and dying, from his rest on the sea-floor,
where he might have lived till the Judgement Day.'[20]
The journalists contemplate their huge 'scoop', then
realize that their editors would disbelieve it, and
regard it as a practical joke. Sadly, they abandon
their plans to report it:

'What are you going to do?'
'Tell it as a lie.'
'Fiction?' This with the full-blooded disgust of a journalist for
    the illegitimate branch of the profession.
'You can call it that if you like. I shall call it a lie.'
And a lie it has become; for Truth is a naked lady, and if by
    accident she is drawn up from the bottom of the sea, it
    behoves a gentleman either to give her a print petticoat or
    to turn his face to the wall and vow that he did not see.[21]

The story of the sea-serpent illustrates a basic
dilemma which all journalists face. They cannot report

everything. This is clearly impossible. But how do they make a selection? They must select not only among the stories, but among the events surrounding the stories, as the next section will discuss. The whole question of 'representation', as the depiction of events by the media is sometimes labelled, has become a key topic in the area known as 'media studies'.[22]

Picking and choosing

'It's hard to explain, but in the process of writing an article, a writer has to pick and choose. He has to edit a person's words, select some quotes and discard others, perhaps even change what a person said to make the meaning clearer. When you do this, it's almost impossible not to change the story in one way or another.'[23]

These lines, said by a journalist in Anita Shreve's novel *Strange fits of passion*, sum up the inevitable modifications that are made as a story is written.

The role of journalists is more complex than might appear at first sight. The simplest view is that they are 'newshounds', skilled hunters and gatherers who are permanently on the lookout for juicy pieces of news, like pigs snuffling for truffles. When they have found some, they dig them out, and transmit the essence to their readers. This viewpoint ties in with their own self-perception: 'Central among journalistic beliefs is the idea of news as random and unpredictable events tracked down by the skills of journalistic anticipation and circumspection.'[24] As C. P. Scott, a long-serving editor of the *Guardian* newspaper (1872–1929), famously said in 1921:

The primary office of a newspaper is the gathering of news. At the peril of its soul it must see that the supply is not tainted. Neither in what it gives, nor in what it does not give, nor in the mode of presentation, must the unclouded face of truth suffer wrong . . . Comment is free, but facts are sacred . . . The voice of opponents no less than that of friends has a right to be heard . . . It is well to be frank, it is even better to be fair.[25]

This simple 'transmission model' suggests that journalists first find important news items, then skilfully transmit them to others. An aeroplane crashes, journalists rush to the scene, and provide details of which aeroplane, where, when, how many people were killed, how and why it happened, as in the 'who, what, where, how, why' scenario outlined in chapter 6.

But this model is over-simple. No journalist, or even group of journalists, could ever cover everything that happens: they have to choose what to report. The selection has to tie in with what both editors and readers find important and interesting. As a first approximation, 'News is anything that makes a reader say "Gee Whiz!"' (chapter 5). But at a less superficial level, news is likely to be events which re-affirm accepted values in the society in which the readers live, for example that murder and theft are wrong, that criminals should be punished, and that children should be looked after. This 'solidarity model' asserts common shared values, and provides a comfortable feeling that the world around is behaving in an orderly fashion. Daily newspapers mostly work with this model, and many politicians try to promote it. As one writer commented: 'News cannot stray too far from what news has been, because news stories must be resonant with the stories that Society believes about itself.'[26] An even stronger 'ritual view' of communication suggests that journalists are essentially engaged in 'the creation, representation, and celebration of shared even if illusory beliefs'.[27]

But even this view may be over-simple: media reports are typically multi-layered confections, as will be outlined below.

Multiple layers

Neither the naive transmission model, nor the more realistic 'solidarity model', outlined in the section above reflects reality. Instead, '"News" is the end-product of a complex process.'[28] At the very least, five layers can be detected behind each news report – and there may be more.

BASIC MODEL	
1. EVENT	e.g. murder
2. DECISION	newsworthy
3. REPORT	'facts' selected
4. HIDDEN MESSAGES	e.g. crime must be punished
5. ASSESSMENT	news + entertainment

First, an event takes place: something happens, maybe a murder. Second, decisions and conventions come into play, which assess whether the event is 'newsworthy' (newsworthiness was discussed in chapter 5). Third, the news report is written, which conveys the selected 'facts'. Fourth, hidden messages are conveyed by the way the facts are described, such as 'crime will be punished'. The fifth layer is the assessment by readers, for example that the report was a worthwhile mix of news and entertainment/titillation.

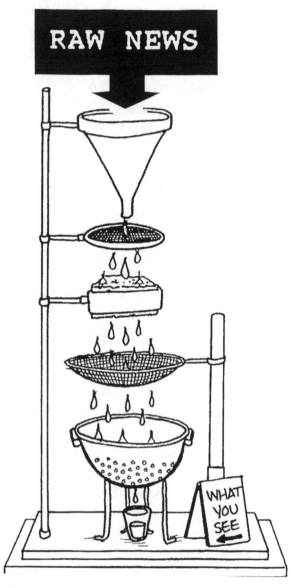

Fig. 10.2. Filtering raw news.

Further messages, not always intended, may be read into the reports by those reading or watching the news, such as 'women are extra guilty if they are involved with murder or a murderer', as appears to have happened in the British Soham case (chapter 6), in which two young children were murdered. The female partner of the murderer received more public hatred than the murderer, even though she had not in fact co-operated in the killing. She had been miles away, visiting her mother, and had merely given her partner a false alibi.[29]

Yet even the five-layer model outlined above may be over-simple. An assessment of a highly publicized American case, that of O.-J. Simpson, a basket-ball hero accused of murdering his girl-friend, suggested that at least eight levels may need to be considered.[30] These extra layers arose because the jury, the media, and the general public probably all had different views on the case, each of which influenced the overall assessment/interpretation. These multiple layers raise further questions, about 'gatekeeping', as will be discussed below.

The gatekeeping problem

'Gatekeeping is the process by which the billions of messages that are available in the world get cut down and transformed into the hundreds of messages that reach a given person on a given day.'[31] A serious question therefore arises: when journalists filter their stories through various layers, do they (or their employers) cynically twist what they are writing, so as

Fig. 10.3. Gatekeeping.

to deceive readers or viewers? Or is such editing an inevitable consequence of the need to make stories clear and coherent?

Vocabulary editing is the most obvious, and most easily detectable type of 'filter'. During political elections, and especially during wars, journalists are even briefed on how to refer to 'them' and 'us':[32] 'they' destroy and kill; 'we' take out, suppress, neutralize, decapitate. 'Our boys' are professional, resolute, brave, loyal heroes. 'Their troops' are brainwashed, ruthless, fanatical, blindly obedient. Andrew Marr comments: 'The columnist will do no good without a decent sense of how to use English unfairly. The cheer-words (decent, fair, reasonable, fresh, open, clear, brave) and the boo-words (biased, sordid, odious, tyrannical) must be carefully assembled, to be rained down on the reader like rocks from an ambush.[33] And the use of metaphor for dehumanizing enemies was pointed out in chapter 9. These vocabulary gimmicks show that readers/viewers should be on their guard, though such usages are easily detectable by intelligent literates.

Presupposition is a slightly less obvious ploy. In July 1991, the journalist Andrew Morton wrote a piece for the *Sunday Times* about the marriage of Prince Charles and Princess Diana 'suggesting that there had been a "truce" between the couple. Writing of a truce is an excellent way of admitting there is a war without actually having to say so.'[34] And as pointed out in chapter 7, presupposition is often built into advertising. Yet again, intelligent readers are likely to be aware of such tricks.

Faking it

More worrying, perhaps, are cases in which journalists are tempted to invent stories. Let us consider why they might do this, and what this tells us about the role of journalism in the current age. The simplest reason for faking it is sheer laziness: 'Old Eddy smiled . . . He dipped his pen in the ink and began to copy out in his close, careful longhand a report which had been published exactly one hundred years ago on Thursday week, about a boiler bursting in Darlington with the loss of thirteen lives.'

These lines come from a novel by the writer
Michael Frayn, *Towards the end of the morning* (1967),[35]
where an ageing journalist is trying to make life easy
for himself. But cutting corners in a busy life may not
be the only reason for invention. In an earlier novel,
The tin men (1965), Frayn, who began his career as a
journalist, satirized the invention of newspaper
stories designed to please.

In his novel, a research institute aims to program
a digital computer to create a fictitious but 'perfectly
satisfactory daily newspaper with all the variety and
news sense of the old hand-made article'.[36] Surveys
were carried out to discover what type of news
stories people liked best:

The crash survey showed that people were not interested
in reading about road crashes unless there were at least ten
dead. A road crash with ten dead, the majority felt, was
slightly less interesting than a rail crash with one dead,
unless it had piquant details – the ten dead turning out to be
five still virginal honeymoon couples, for example . . . A rail
crash was always entertaining, with or without children's
toys still lying pathetically among the wreckage . . . But
people really preferred an air crash . . . What people
enjoyed most was about 70 dead, with some 20 survivors
including children rescued after at least one night
in open boats.[37]

A murder questionnaire asked readers how they liked
their murders: 'Do you prefer to read about murders in
which the victim is (a) a small girl (b) an old lady (c) an
illegitimately pregnant young woman (d) a prostitute
(e) a Sunday school teacher?'[38] Another question asked
about the dress, or undress, of the victim: 'Do you

prefer a female victim to be naked, or to be clad in
underclothes?'

Another question was about the method of death:
'Do you prefer the victim to have been (a) shot (b)
strangled (c) stabbed (d) beaten to death (e) kicked to
death (f) left to die of exposure?' Once these surveys
had been completed, and the results made known to
the staff, then they could fashion their stories in
accordance with their readers' preferences, and the
modern newspaper's 'last residual connection with the
raw, messy, offendable real world would have been
broken'.[39]

Some recent scandals, with faked or plagiarized
newspaper reports, show that the temptation to fake
sensational stories is a permanent problem. Michael
Finkel was fired from the *New York Times Magazine* in
2002 because the central character in his cover story
about poverty and exploitation in the Ivory Coast was a
deliberate invention. Finkel's character Youssouf was
compounded from the real stories of a number of
different impoverished West African boys. Finkel felt
his story answered a higher truth than mere factual
accuracy. His article, he asserted, was true in spirit,
and he deluded himself that this was all the
truth that mattered.[40]

The year after the Finkel fiasco, the *New York Times*
itself was hit by a far worse fraud problem. A key
reporter, Jayson Blair, had developed a drink and drugs
problem at college. The strains of his career led him
to use even more drugs and booze, he claimed. An
inquiry was launched after complaints from staff and
readers that some of his stories appeared to be copied

from other newspapers: 'A huge internal investigation uncovered serial fraud. Blair made up stories and sources, invented interview subjects and often wrote stories claiming to be from far-flung parts of America when in fact he had not left his Brooklyn apartment.'[41]

In the same year, 'America's media, already reeling from the Jayson Blair plagiarism scandal, has been rocked by the revelation that yet another top reporter has been making up news stories.'[42] Jack Kelley, senior foreign correspondent for *USA Today* had been faking major foreign news stories for several years. Kelley claimed that he saw three men have their heads blown off in a suicide bombing in Jerusalem. 'In a first draft of his piece he described how the heads rolled "with their eyes still blinking". However, police records show that no adult victims of the blast were decapitated.'[43]

The fakers in these cases were rightly censured. But in other cases, the situation is less clear, especially in a culture where imagination is so highly prized, and where the 'truth' is often hard to seek out.

'There is a simple view of my trade. Good journalists are those who get it right; bad journalists are those who get it wrong. Impossible to argue with that, you think? Well, let me try', says John Humphrys.

Bad journalists never let the facts get in the way of a story. They decide what the story is going to be, manufacture enough material to make it look plausible and run with it. There is usually a kernel of truth buried somewhere, but you need to look hard to find it and most casual readers have neither the time nor the inclination . . . But beyond that it

starts to get difficult. Good journalists tell the truth,
pure and simple . . . The problem with the simple view
of journalism is that it is no good saying we must report
only what is true because what is true cannot always be
proven.[44]

Political sleaze stories, for example, are invariably
denied when they are first reported. Later, they are
often found to be right. Humphrys concludes: 'One of
the trickiest areas in any democracy is finding the
right balance between the power and the responsibility
of the media . . . But what we should always keep in
the back of our minds is that even the best journalists
must sometimes be free to be wrong.'

If journalists provide fictionalized or wrong
reports, this raises a serious question. What is the role
of newspapers, or other media, in the current age? Do
they really exist in order to provide the public with
entertaining fiction, as Frayn's satire suggests? As long
ago as 1961, the American writer Philip Roth suggested
that newspapers might be replacing novels:

He [Roth] made a statement that had a terrific impact on
other young writers. We now live in an age, he said, in which
the imagination of the novelist lies helpless before what he
knows he will read in tomorrow morning's newspaper. The
actuality is continually outdoing our talents, and the culture
tosses up figures daily that are the envy of any novelist.[45]

Tom Wolfe wrote this in the preface to his novel *The
bonfire of the vanities* (1987). He continued:

Even today – perhaps especially today [1987] – anyone, writer
or not can sympathize. What novelist would dare concoct a
plot in which, say, a Southern television evangelist has a tryst
in a hotel with a church secretary from Babylon, New

York – Did you have to make it *Babylon*? – and is ruined to the point where he has to sell all his worldly goods at auction, including his air-conditioned doghouse.

Wolfe argued: 'Of one thing I am sure. If fiction writers do not start facing the obvious, the literary history of the second half of the twentieth century will record that journalists not only took over the richness of American life as their only domain but also seized the high ground of literature itself.'[46]

Piers Morgan would agree. For ten years (from 1994) he was a successful editor of the London-based *News of the World*, and then the *Daily Mirror* (two high-selling British tabloids). He believes that highlighting horrors is what people want from journalists. According to a profile of Morgan in a British Sunday newspaper, he claimed that to be successful 'a modern British tabloid paper has to shout loud and long to stand even the remotest chance of being heard . . . "I think in the modern commercial world it's not enough for newspapers to sit back and cover news in the way they used to . . . You have to be a scoop-led newspaper to generate excitement in your product and to drive sales."'[47] In his own book, *The insider* (2005), he stated: 'I always viewed editing a tabloid as an instinctive, high-octane, dangerous and ultimately short-lived pursuit. A bit like flying a fighter jet . . . Eventually, the chances are that you're going to crash and burn. But what a ride while it lasts!'[48]

John Carey suggests that more may be at stake than mere excitement. He claims that reportage (newspaper reporting in a wide sense) has taken over from religion. In the past 'religion was the permanent backdrop to his [a person's] existence, as reportage is for his modern counterpart',[49] he suggests. Reportage supplies a constant and reassuring sense of events going on beyond a person's immediate horizon, he argues. When the events are terrible, they contrast more comfortingly with the reader's supposed safety:

> Reportage, taking religion's place, endlessly feeds its reader with accounts of the deaths of other people, and therefore places him continually in the position of a survivor – one who has escaped the violent and terrible ends which, it graphically apprises him, others have come to. In this way reportage, like religion, gives the individual a comforting sense of his own immortality.[50]

Various other views are found as to what might be taking the place of religion. The novelist David Lodge has suggested that the package sightseeing tour might be replacing pilgrimage, and rejuvenating breaks be taking the place of religious retreats.[51]

Yet to many people reportage in newspapers may be becoming less important than gossip and shopping, as will be outlined below.

Solidarity

Celebrity gossip has largely taken over from shock-horror stories (chapter 5), except in extreme cases, such as mega-disasters, and horrific crimes. This may seem trivial to serious readers. But, as already noted (chapter 5), it serves a serious (though not usually identified purpose) in that it gives readers a comfortable feeling of solidarity with each other, and with society: 'you too could be there'. Such gossip promotes an illusion that a glamorous life-style is within reach of everyone, it just needs a little luck (particularly financial), and a small amount of effort.

Bridging the gap between an ordinary and a celebrity life-style, the media imply, is primarily a matter of 'dressing the part'. Andrew Marr argues: 'Today perhaps the biggest new area of mass reporting is simply shopping – "news" as thinly disguised advertising . . . Editors believe that the British today are most interested in their number-one leisure activity: buying stuff. So shopping mad have we become as a society that the adverts . . . are now becoming the news'.[52] In a relatively affluent society, many of us rely on the media for suggestions on what to buy, whether it is clothes, books, food or furniture. We do not want to change, which makes for a stable society, and we may even make donations (about perhaps the same amount as the cost of a pair of new shoes) to disaster funds in other parts of the world.

In short, newspapers – and other media – always have been, and maybe always will be, a mixture of news and entertainment: part horror-comics (when disasters strike), part gossip-mongers (when celebrities marry and split up), part shopping aids (a solidarity ploy in a prosperous society).

Final words

The media are here to stay, and so is literature – though their format will undoubtedly alter over the years, and new technologies will come to the fore. Kate Adie, for many years the BBC's chief news correspondent, regards herself as 'a privileged gnat alighting on the faces of history, part of events great and small'.[53] She concludes: 'How we see our world and tell others about it will always be changing. Fashion and commerce modify the menu and the style, and technology galvanises the speed of delivery and the spread of information. The printing press and the satellite alter the means; education regulates the understanding.'[54] Television is watched by most people, mobile phones with text messaging are on the increase, and online news is proliferating.[55] Newspapers are reportedly on the decline, though several new London newspapers are distributed free. They are widely read and appreciated by those who find then. As one journalist, Raymond Snoddy, noted: 'My favourite media myth . . . is the utter failure of newspapers to collapse and disappear as they were supposed to.'[56] Similarly, another, Peter Preston, has argued: 'Reports of our death have been exaggerated.' He points out: 'The most consistent headline story is one of titles increasing in number, while their pagination goes on swelling.'[57]

This book has shown that so-called 'news' always was and possibly always will be a complex mix of information and entertainment. Those who condemn newspapers and other media are usually avid media devourers who have failed to understand that they not only contain an account of recent happenings, but encapsulate our own beliefs about ourselves and our culture. As Michael Schudson,

Professor of Communication and Sociology at the University of California, San Diego, pointed out:

few things are more characteristic and more revealing of modern culture than the invention of and changes in the way it declares itself anew each day in its presentation of news. The world may be 'out there,' as so many of us commonsensically believe. But no person and no instrument apprehends it directly. We turn nature to culture as we talk and write and narrate it.[58]

The same insight was expressed perhaps more neatly by the playwright Arthur Miller: 'A good newspaper, I suppose, is a nation talking to itself.'[59]

Epilogue

This book began with a paradox. Both journalists (newshounds) and literary writers (wordsmiths) are skilled word weavers. Yet the former are typically heavily criticized, and the latter are often highly praised, even though the moaned-about journalists are far more widely read than the eulogized literary writers. As chapter 1 explained, this book explores this puzzle.

Chapter 2 looked at oral performance, which antedated written language by tens of thousands of years, and provided the foundation on which later literature was (often unknowingly) based. Chapter 3 outlined the invention of writing, and discussed the relationship between spoken and written language.

Chapter 4 explored the descendants of the earlier oral tradition, which were also the predecessors of modern newspapers: broadside ballads, chapbooks and newsbooks.

Chapter 5 outlined the development of daily newspapers. Chapter 6 showed that modern newspapers continue a long-standing tradition of story-telling. It sketched the conventions which underlie modern news stories. Chapter 7 pointed out the high polish of much journalism, and outlined the writing guidelines typically followed.

Chapter 8 looked at the language of poetry, another type of highly polished creativity. Chapter 9 explored metaphor. It enumerated the various uses of metaphor and compared and contrasted metaphor in newspapers with metaphor in poetry.

Chapter 10 outlined some of the conventions and aims of journalism, and showed how they differ from those of literary language. It reiterated that the work of newshounds and that of wordsmiths is worthwhile, but that journalism needs to be more widely recognized as both valuable and highly skilled.

NOTES

When two dates appear side by side, the first is the original date of a quotation, and the second is a more accessible reprint.

Unless otherwise indicated, 'Aitchison' in citations refers to Jean Aitchison.

1 Weaving and worrying

1 Shaw 1977:71.
2 Lear 1871/1994:183.
3 Borges 1969/1974:27. Borges quotes Sir Walter Scott's *Demonology and witchcraft* as his source for banshees.
4 Shakespeare, *Antony and Cleopatra*, 4.xii.2–6.
5 Humboldt 1836/1988:215.
6 Hockett 1958:585.
7 Pinker 1994:19.
8 Saussure 1915/1959:10.
9 Coppens 1994, Aitchison 1996/2000.
10 Jackendoff 1999, 2002.
11 Mellars 1993.
12 John Keats, 'Ode to a nightingale' in Keats 1908:230.
13 Nottebohm 1975.
14 Au 1993.
15 Goodall 1986:125.

16 Ogden Nash, 'Where there's a will, there's a velleity' in Nash 1985:144.

17 Gleitman *et al.* 1972:160.

18 Karmiloff-Smith 1992:31.

19 Jennings 1989:74.

20 T. S. Eliot, 'East Coker' lines 70–1, in Eliot 1949.

21 T. S. Eliot, 'Burnt Norton', lines 149–53, in Eliot 1949.

22 Matthew Arnold, quoted at www.quotegarden.com/ journalism.html. This presumed Arnold quotation occurs repeatedly in journalism, though its exact source is elusive.

23 Ezra Pound 1931, in Crystal and Crystal 2000:237.

24 Oliver Goldsmith in 'Poetry distinguished from other writing', in *Essays* no.15 (1758–65), in Crystal and Crystal 2000:242.

25 J. Raymond 1993:xviii.

26 Sheridan 1779/1988:1.1.

27 Coleridge, *Biographia Literaria*, published between 1808 and 1815, quoted by Sampson 1996/1999, in Tumber 1999:202.

28 In Snoddy 1992:21.

29 In Bailey 1992:241.

30 In Bailey 1992:242.

31 In Wilkes 2002:2.

32 In Parris 1994:134.

33 Cyril Connolly 1938 in Crystal and Crystal 2000:235.

34 The quotes are from Parris 1994:133–4.

35 Bellow 1961/2001:34.

36 *Observer*, 29 December 2002.

37 Marr 2004/2005:377.

2 Singers of tales

1 Lord 1960/2000:124.

2 Proverbs 4.5.

3 Ecclesiastes 12.9.

4 Aitchison 1996/2000, 2001.

5 Campanile 1987:26, translated in Watkins 1995:69.
6 Beekes 1995, Mallory 1989, Thième 1964.
7 Watkins 1995.
8 Homer, *Odyssey* 2.75.
9 Ayto 1990, under *cattle*.
10 Homer, *Iliad* 8.143.
11 Watkins 1995.
12 *Iliad* 16.856–7 (death of Patroklos) = *Iliad* 22.362–3 (death of Hector) discussed in Watkins 1995:499.
13 *Beowulf* 2819–20.
14 Watkins 1995:24.
15 Watkins 1995.
16 *Iliad* 2.538.
17 *Iliad* 2.582.
18 *Iliad* 2.712.
19 *Odyssey* 8.43f.
20 *Odyssey* 8.79–80.
21 Ong 1988/2002:22.
22 Rudyard Kipling, 'When 'Omer smote 'is bloomin' lyre', in Kipling 1940:351.
23 Ong 1988/2002:23.
24 Rudyard Kipling 'In the Neolithic age', in Kipling 1940:343.
25 Parry 1930/1971:266–324.
26 *Odyssey* 8.79–80.
27 *Iliad* 6.152–5.
28 *Odyssey* 8.326–7.
29 Ong 1988/2002:34.
30 Kirk 1985:xxiii, cf. West 1988.
31 *Iliad* 22.93–5.
32 *Odyssey* 8.305–6.
33 *Odyssey* 6.137.
34 Aitchison 1963.
35 *Iliad* 2.89.
36 *Rig Veda* 28.7.
37 *Odyssey* 10.449.
38 *Iliad* 10.542.
39 *Iliad* 13.484.

40 *Odyssey* 11.320.
41 Tennyson, 'Lady Clara Vere-de-Vere' ii.
42 Joni Mitchell, 'In France they kiss on main street', on *The hissing of summer lawns*.
43 Aitchison 1964.
44 Ong 1988/2002:26.
45 Ong 1988/2002:26.
46 S. Johnson 1775/1996:98–9.
47 S. Johnson 1775/1996:102.
48 S. Johnson 1775/1996:101.
49 S. Johnson 1775/1996:101.
50 Chapman 1992:103.
51 Child 1882–98/1965.
52 G. L. Kittredge, in Child 1882–98/1965:xxviii.
53 Child 1882–98/1965:55.
54 Child 1882–98/1965:55.

3 The tongue of the hand

1 Henry Ward Beecher, in Crystal and Crystal 2000:107.
2 Abbé de l'Epée, in Sacks 1989/1991:16–17.
3 Rée 1999.
4 Klima and Bellugi 1979, Kyle and Woll 1985, Lane 1984, Sacks 1989/1991.
5 Aitchison 1998.
6 J. P. Hughes 1994:664.
7 Coulmas 1996:376.
8 Gelb 1963:27.
9 Gelb 1963:28.
10 John Bulwer, *Chirologia* (1644), in Butterworth 1999:218.
11 Schaller 1991:61.
12 Butterworth 1999:23.
13 Marshack 1991.
14 Schmandt-Besserat 1978/1986, 1992.
15 Schmandt-Besserat 1978/1986:33.
16 Schmandt-Besserat 1978/1986:35.

17 Schmandt-Besserat 1978/1986:35.
18 Schmandt-Besserat 1978/1986:37.
19 Schmandt-Besserat 1978/1986:37.
20 Coe 1992/1994, Coulmas 1996.
21 Chadwick 1958:81. The script of Mycenaean was known as Linear B before it was deciphered. For clear information on Linear B and writing in general, see Robinson 1995, 2002.
22 *Longman dictionary of the English language* (1984).
23 John and Blake 2001.
24 Gray 2000:39.
25 Diringer 1968.
26 Diringer 1962:14.
27 Milne 1926/1978:73.
28 Charles Dickens, *Great Expectations* (1860–1), chapter 7.
29 Saussure 1915/1959:51.
30 Trench 1856:207.
31 *Ghoti* for 'fish' is popularly attributed to Bernard Shaw, but Shaw's biographer, Michael Holroyd, casts doubt on this: Holroyd 1991:501. The spelling of 'orthography' is in Ellis 1845:16, fn.4.
32 From 'A play on words' attributed to Eugene Field 1850–95 in Silcock 1952:218.
33 Anon., referred to as an 'old chestnut' in the *Author* 103, 3, Autumn 2002:135. This is only one of several versions of this verse which are in circulation.
34 Dukes 2002:3.
35 Swift 1712.
36 *Sunday Times* 'Doors' section, 22 December 2002.
37 Hanna *et al.* 1966. Also Carney 1994, Rollings 2004.
38 *Guardian* 'Online' section 14 November 2002.
39 John and Blake 2001.
40 Jeremy Clarkson in the *Sunday Times*, 29 August 2004.
41 Saussure 1915/1959:23.
42 Lyons 1968:39.
43 Saussure 1915/1959:25.
44 Richard Chenevix Trench 1855. Also quoted in Crystal and Crystal 2000:112.

45 Tannen 1989:55.
46 Elman *et al.* 1996:2.
47 Derrida 1967/1997:36.
48 Biber 1988, 1995, Biber *et al.* 1998, 1999.
49 Snowling 1987.
50 J. Marshall 1976.
51 Coltheart *et al.* 1987.

4 Hangings, histories, marvels, mysteries

1 William Brown 1616, in Watt 1991:24.
2 Shepherd 1969:14. See also Shepherd 1962.
3 Watt 1991:11.
4 Shakespeare, *A winter's tale*, 4.iii.261f.
5 Watt 1991:166.
6 O'Connell 1999:90.
7 Chappell 1859/1965:387.
8 Child 1882–98/1965:III (1888), 56, no.117.
9 Child 1882–98/1965:III (1888), 106–7, no.120B.
10 Child 1882–98/1965:III (1888), 372, no.170.
11 Lloyd 1967:147.
12 Lloyd 1967:147.
13 Child 1882–98/1965:III (1888), 372.
14 Watt 1991:42.
15 Watt 1991:42.
16 Watt 1991:11.
17 Puttenham 1589/1970. *The art of poesie* was written around 1570, though published later, in 1589.
18 Watt 1991:43.
19 Watt 1991:264. Watt counted those mentioned in Shaaber 1929.
20 *OED* (= *Oxford English Dictionary*) under *chapman*.
21 Watt 1991:291.
22 Watt 1991:294.
23 Watt 1991:292.
24 Watt 1991:312.

25 Watt 1991:266.
26 *OED* under *courant*.
27 Jonson's address 'to the readers' is in the 1631 publication of his 1626 play: Jonson 1631/1988:152–3.
28 Shaaber 1929:1.
29 *OED* under *news*.
30 *OED* under *news*.
31 *OED* under *news*.
32 Shakespeare, *Richard III*, 4.iv.457.
33 Jonson 1631/1988:1.v.48–9.
34 *OED* under *news*.
35 *OED* under *news*.
36 *OED* under *news*.
37 S. Johnson 1755/1990.
38 Raymond 1993:33–4.
39 Extracts from *A Perfect Diurnall of the Passages of Parliament*, 18–25 July 1642, in Raymond 1993:57–8.
40 Extracts from *A Perfect Diurnall of Some Passages in Parliament*, 30 December – 6 January 1644, in Raymond 1993:301–2.
41 *Mercurius Publicus* 17, 19–26 April 1660, in Raymond 1993:454.
42 *Mercurius Aulicus*, 17–23 December 1643, in Raymond 1993:106.
43 *The Weekly Intelligencer of the Common-Wealth* 12, 19–26 July 1659, in Raymond 1993:422.
44 *A Perfect Account*, 17–24 January 1654, in Raymond 1993:127.
45 *Mercurius Politicus* 179, 10–17 November 1653, in Raymond 1993:311.
46 *The Loyall Scout* 17, 19–26 August 1659, in Raymond 1993:439.
47 Raymond 1993:13–14.
48 Raymond 1993:14.

5 Calendars of roguery and woe

1 Bulwer-Lytton 1840/1953:47. I am grateful to Laurel Brake of Birkbeck College, University of London, for pointing out this quotation.

2 Goldsmith 1762.

3 Crabbe 1785 quoted in Engel 1996:19.

4 Grant 1871:3. The passages describing the history of *The Times* are from Grant 1871, unless otherwise stated. Any unreferenced quotation refers to the same page as the previous quotation. Curran and Seaton (2003) contains a useful general bibliography on press history, divided into topics. Griffiths 2006 is an authoritative survey of 500 years of Fleet Street history. Also useful is Greenslade 2003/2004. Marr 2004/2005 is a readable account written by a reliable 'hands-on' journalist. Conboy 2002, 2004, 2006 and Horrie 2003 contain useful overviews of the tabloid press. Randall 2005 provides profiles of notable male journalists, and Mill and Cochrane 2005 have assembled a collection of outstanding work by female journalists. Other noteworthy books on journalism will be referenced in chapters 6, 7 and 10.

5 Grant 1971:4.

6 Circulation figures quoted by Grant 1871 were taken by him from the *Encyclopaedia Britannica*.

7 Grant 1871:13.

8 Grant 1871:53.

9 Grant 1871:22.

10 Grant 1871:23.

11 Grant 1871:91.

12 Grant 1871:92.

13 Grant 1871:93.

14 Grant 1871:97.

15 Engel 1996:37.

16 Engel 1996:38.

17 Engel, ibid.

18 Engel 1996:40.

19 Doyle 1892/1981:249 in 'The adventure of the blue carbuncle'.

20 Engel 1996:17.

21 Engel 1996:17. The rhyme provided the journalist Matthew Engel with the title of his book *Tickle the public* (1996), which outlines one hundred years of the popular press.

22 Keimer, quoted in Wilkes 2002:87.
23 The definition quoted is from *The new shorter Oxford dictionary* (1993), and is a typical dictionary definition of *news*.
24 Quoted in Boyd 1994:3, and sometimes attributed to the American newspaper editor Arthur McEwan.
25 Sommerville 1996:4.
26 Quoted in Wilkes 2002:83.
27 Jean Anouilh, *La répétition*, Act 3 (1950), http://en.thinkexist. com/quotes/jean_anouilh/4.html.
28 Nevinson 1925:177.
29 Herbert 1931:412–13.
30 Engel 1996:129.
31 Bell 1991:55.
32 Galtung and Ruge 1965/1999:21.
33 Marr 2004/2005:60.
34 Palmer 1978:216.
35 Marr 2004/5:114.
36 Jonson 1631/1988:3.iii.46–8.
37 *Review*, 19 September 1704, quoted in Wilkes 2002:21.
38 Sheridan 1777/8, in 1988:1.i.
39 Lamb 1833/n.d.:299–302.
40 Waugh 1930/1938:50.
41 Wilkes 2002:161.
42 Wilkes 2002:3.
43 Wilkes 2002:275.
44 Wilkes 2002:276.
45 Wilkes 2002:288.
46 Wilkes 2002:9.
47 Wilkes 2002:322.
48 Wilkes 2002:323.
49 *Daily Star*, 26 February 2004.
50 *Sun*, 26 February 2004.
51 *News of the World*, 25 July 2004.
52 Nash 1985:375.
53 Marr 2004/2005:115.
54 Professor Geoffrey Beattie of Manchester University, quoted by Liz Hoggard in article 'Celebrity gossip is good for your health', *Observer*, 16 May 2004.

6 Story-telling

1 Bell 1991:147. Also in Graddol and Boyd-Barrett 1994:100. Bell was one of the first to explain the work of journalists in a way recognized by non-journalists. Cotter 2001 contains further insightful comments. Numerous useful 'how to' books are also worth consulting, e.g. Bagnall 1993, Boyd 1994, Burns 2002, Harcup 2004.

2 Paul Hoggart, *The Times*, 12 March 2004. The children were Holly Wells and Jessica Chapman.

3 Bell 1991:147.

4 Waugh 1938/1943:21.

5 Waugh 1938/1943:146.

6 *Sunday Times*, 12 February 2004.

7 Kipling 1940:606.

8 James Aitchison 1988:22.

9 *The Times*, 19 February 2004.

10 *Sunday Times*, 7 April 1996.

11 *People*, 1 February 2004.

12 *The Times*, 1 September 1888. Also at www.historybuff.com/library/refLT9188.html.

13 *Guardian*, 19 May 1995.

14 This diagram is simplified from one in Bell 1991:171.

15 *The Times*, 16 July 2004.

16 Fedler *et al.* 2001:200.

17 Fedler *et al.* 2001:208.

18 Simon Garfield, *OM* (= *Observer Monthly*), 18 July 2004, pp. 25–32.

19 Aitchison and Lewis 2003a:2.

20 Article headed 'Voices from beneath an icy wasteland' by Victor Saunders, *Observer*, 14 February 1999, p. 25.

21 Article headed 'Tourist massacre plunges heart of Africa into deeper darkness' by Jon Swain, *Sunday Times*, 7 March 1999.

22 Article headed 'Chasm at quake's epicentre' by John Arlidge, *Observer*, 29 August 1999.

23 Article headed 'Coastlines of devastation' by David Williams, *Daily Mail*, 27 December 2004.

24 *Daily Mail*, 24 October 1896, in Marr 2004/2005:80.
25 *Daily Mail*, 31 August 2005.
26 Aitchison 2003a.
27 Douglas Fraser, *Sunday Herald*, 30 September 2001.
28 Michael Ellison and Ed Vulliamy, *Guardian*, 12 September 2001.
29 The comments and conclusions about 11 September (originally in Aitchison 2003a) are based on a *Guardian Special* which reprinted over twenty separate accounts and comments originally published in the *Guardian*; a BBC book which contained fifteen papers assessing and analysing the events (Baxter and Downing 2001); and miscellaneous reports from newspapers and the Web in the days and weeks following 9/11.
30 Haiman 1985, Nänny and Fischer 1999.
31 Fergal Keane, in Baxter and Downing 2001:62.
32 Orla Guerin, in Baxter and Downing 2001:144.
33 These layered (once known as 'weakened') meanings are from the British National Corpus.
34 Baxter and Downing 2001, F. Halliday 2002.
35 Ayto 1999:279.
36 Butler, quoted in Crystal and Crystal 2000:188.

7 Glimmering words

1 Joel Chandler Harris in Boyd 1994:52.
2 Preston 1999/2000:54–5.
3 Anon., quoted by Adam Brewer, 21 August 1987, in a letter to *The Times*, in Crystal and Crystal 2000:275.
4 Orwell 1946/1962:156.
5 Orwell 1946/1962:157.
6 Orwell 1946/1962:156.
7 Maugham quoted in Evans 2000:75.
8 Evans 2000:75.
9 Taylor 1991:283.
10 Taylor 1991:282.

11 Ian Rankin, *Knots and crosses*. London: Orion Books, 1987/1998, p. 92.

12 Crystal and Davy 1969, though outdated in places, still contains useful comments about newspaper style.

13 *Daily Mail*, 30 July 2005, p. 2.

14 *Daily Mail*, 30 July 2005, p. 5.

15 *Daily Mail*, 30 July 2005, p. 4.

16 *Daily Mail*, 30 July 2005, p. 4.

17 Some of these (from the 1990s) were pointed out by Bell 1991:196, others are from relatively recent (2005) newspapers.

18 Ni 2003.

19 Biber 2003:170.

20 Marr 2004/2005:225.

21 Frayn 1965/1995:59–60.

22 Headlines are discussed in Bell 1991, Kniffka 1980, Mardh 1980, Schneider 2000, Simon-Vandenbergen 1981, van Dijk 1988.

23 van Dijk 1988:189.

24 *Sunday Times*, 28 July 2003.

25 *Daily Star*, 18 August 1999.

26 *Newham Recorder*, 16 March 2005.

27 Taylor 1991:291.

28 *Sun*, 22 October 1999.

29 *Mirror*, 3 November 2000.

30 *Sun*, 21 August 2003.

31 Swan 1995:359–69.

32 Examples from Crystal 1998:201.

33 These headlines were all from newspapers on 8 July 2005, the day after the outrage.

34 Engel 1996:28.

35 Sugden 1995:59.

36 Sugden 1995:73.

37 Schneider 2000:54.

38 The headlines relating to the murdered French student are from the *Electronic Telegraph*, between Christmas and New Year 1996.

39 *Sun*, 22 October 1999.

40 Simon-Vandenbergen 1981.

41 February–July 1992, Aitchison, Lewis and Naylor 2000.

42 Aitchison 1996/2000.

43 Home Office 1992.

44 M. A. K. Halliday 1994.

45 Scotts of Stowe Spring/Summer Catalogue 2004.

46 Addison, 13 September 1710, 'Advertisements', *Tatler*, 224, quoted in Crystal and Crystal 2000:275, 59.1.

47 On advertising, see Cook 2001, Myers 1994, 1999, Tanaka 1994, Vestergaard and Schrøder 1985.

48 Neff ceramic hob ad, *Woman and Home*, October 2004.

49 'Nutrasome' is a Revlon product.

8 Painting with words

1 Shakespeare, *A midsummer night's dream*, 5.i.12–17.

2 W. B. Yeats, 'Adam's curse' (1904) in Yeats 1990.

3 Seamus Heaney, 'Digging' in Heaney 1990:1.

4 *Audacht Morainn* (seventh-century Early Irish) quoted in Watkins 1995:262.

5 Bradford 1996a:3. Other definitions/discussions of poetry are found in numerous places, eg. Fenton 2002, Furniss and Bath 1996, Roberts 2000. For 'cognitive poetics' which links more closely with stylistics (literary linguistics), see Gavins and Steen 2003, Stockwell 2002.

6 A. E. Houseman in Koestler 1978:319.

7 Koestler 1978:319.

8 Walter de la Mare, 'Silver' in de la Mare 1913/1955.

9 Opie and Opie 1951/1997:265.

10 Sabine Baring-Gould 1865, hymn 164, *The Lutheran hymnal* (1941).

11 W. H. Auden, 'Night mail' in Auden 1976.

12 Samuel Butler (1612–80), *Hudibras* II, Canto 1, 457, in Crystal and Crystal 2000:240.

13 'Don't ask me', in Thomas 2000:69.

14 'From a play', in William Carlos Williams 1988:45.
15 Wilbur 1973, 2005.
16 'Poeta fit, non nascitur', in Carroll 1939/1982:790–3.
17 For an outline of language structure plus further references, see Aitchison 2003d. The layers of language in relation to stylistics (literary linguistics) are also discussed in, e.g., Simpson 2004.
18 Alfred Lord Tennyson, 'The princess' (1947), Song 3.
19 Rhodes 1994.
20 Tennyson, 'The gardner's daughter', in *English idylls and other poems* (1842).
21 Shakespeare, *Love's labour lost*, 5.ii.925–7.
22 Shakespeare, *The winter's tale*, 5.ii.9.
23 Rhodes 1994:279.
24 John Keats, 'Ode to a nightingale', VI.7–8.
25 George McDonald (1824–1905), 'The wind and the moon', in Philip 1996:64–5.
26 Opie and Opie 1951/1997:174.
27 Further examples of English rhyming formation can be found in Hock and Joseph 1996:169.
28 Robert Browning (1880–9), *The Pied Piper of Hamelin*, stanza iv.
29 Shakespeare, *Henry VI*, 4.i.72.
30 Chapman 1984:148.
31 Alfred Noyes, 'The highwayman', in Philip 1996:147.
32 Eve Merriam, 'Weather', in Philip 1996:223.
33 Lear 1871/1994:273.
34 Coleridge 1993:205. Information on Kubla Khan and Xanadu can be found in Brewer 2005.
35 Paulin 1999:51.
36 Shelley, in Keegan 2000/2001:641.
37 John Agard, 'The wanted man', in Agard 1985:44.
38 R. S. Thomas, 'Vocabulary', in Thomas 2000:63.
39 MacIeish quote from 'Apologia', in Andrews 1996:350.
40 Bradford 1996a:5.
41 Jakobson 1958/1996:17.
42 Jakobson 1958/1996:17.

43 Masefield 1984/1988:144.
44 Tannen 1989:71.
45 Tannen 1989:83.
46 Aitchison 1994.
47 Keats, 'Hyperion', Bk 1, l.1–10, in Keats 1908:248.
48 Aitchison 2003b, Lyons 1968.
49 Ted Hughes, 'The thought-fox', in T. Hughes 1957.
50 Ted Hughes, 'Witches', in T. Hughes 1960.
51 Aitchison 2003b.
52 Ted Hughes, 'Thrushes', in T. Hughes (1960).
53 Thom Gunn, 'The produce district', in Summerfield 1974:80.

9 Two ideas for one

1 Douglas Dunn, 'On roofs of Terry Street', in Dunn 1986. Also in Keegan 2000/2001:1015.
2 In James Boswell, *The life of Samuel Johnson* (1791), ch. 41, quoted in Crystal and Crystal 2000:247.
3 Aristotle, *De arte poetica*, 1457b.
4 Dorothy Parker, American wit (1893–1967). Quoted in Sherrin 2001:59.
5 In older terminology (Richards 1936), the 'target' and 'source' domains were referred to as the 'tenor' and the 'vehicle'.
6 Eward Smith Ufford (1884).
7 Shakespeare, *Timon of Athens*, 5.i.208.
8 G. Lakoff and Johnson 1980:3. Numerous more recent books on metaphor are in line with their approach, for example Gibbs 1994, Goatly 1997, Kittay 1987, Kövesces 1988, 2000, 2002, Ortony 1993, Steen 1994.
9 Reddy 1979/1993. My examples are not necessarily taken from the sources quoted.
10 Lakoff and Johnson 1980:51.
11 Lakoff and Johnson 1980:4.
12 M. Johnson 1987.

13 'Country house prices rocketing', *Sunday Times*,
   16 January 2000.
14 *Guardian*, 6 January 1998.
15 Aitchison 1996/2000.
16 Smith, Pollio and Pitts 1981.
17 Kövesces 2000, 2002, Lakoff and Johnson 1980, Lakoff and
   Turner 1989.
18 Lakoff 1987.
19 Aitchison 2003b.
20 La Mettrie 1748/1912:141, quoted in Mac Cormac 1985:11.
21 Hephzibah Anderson, in the *Observer Technology Magazine*,
   1, July 2005:46.
22 *Scientific American*, 292.2, February 2005.
23 *Concise Oxford Dictionary*, 7th edn (1982).
24 Rosch 1975.
25 Aitchison 1992.
26 Geeraerts 1989.
27 The *OED* attributes this quote to Marchioness Dufferin,
   Vice-regal life in India (1887).
28 Oliver Goldsmith, quoted in Crystal and Crystal 2000:246–7.
29 A. A. Gill, *Sunday Times*, 26 December 1993.
30 Cosmo Landesmann, *Sunday Times*, 11 January 1998.
31 *Observer*, 11 January 1998.
32 *Guardian*, 6 January 1998.
33 *Observer*, 18 January 1997.
34 Robert Harris, *Sunday Times*, 8 December 1996.
35 De Waal 2005:55.
36 Collected by Frank Knowles, Aston University, in Knowles
   1996.
37 The collection is attributed to Antoinette Renouf by
   Rowan 1998.
38 Ben MacIntyre, *The Times*, 29 July 2005.
39 Elgin 1993:146.
40 Trim 1998.
41 Trim 1998 (translation from Italian).
42 Cohn 1987/1989:55.
43 Cohn 1987/1989:55.

44 Aitchison 1997, 2003b.
45 Adam Lindsay Gordon (1833–70), *Ye wearie wayfarer*, Fytte 8.
46 Shakespeare, *Macbeth*, 5.v.21–2.
47 John Dryden, 'Palamon and Arcite'.
48 Emily Dickinson, discussed in Lakoff and Turner 1989.
49 Robert Frost, 'The road not taken' in Frost 1971:205.
50 Dante, *Divina Commedia*, 'Inferno', i.1.
51 Aitchison 2003b.
52 Seamus Heaney, 'The first kingdom' in Heaney 1990:195.
53 Philip Larkin, 'Coming' in Larkin 1973:538.
54 Geeraerts 1989.
55 Carey 2005.
56 Craig Raine, 'A journey to Greece' in Raine 2000:109.
57 Craig Raine, 'On the perpetuum mobile' in Raine 2000:46.
58 Roger McGough, 'Snowscene' in McGough 1989/1990:67.
59 Roger McGough, 'Melting into the foreground' in McGough 1989/1990:218.
60 Sheridan 1779/1988:1.ii.

10 The role of journalism

1 Samuel Coleridge, Letter II in Griggs, 1956–71/2000:II, 616, 13 February 1801.
2 *Sunday Times*, 3 August 2003.
3 J. Lewis 2003:1.
4 Dickens, 'Down with the tide' in *Household Words*, 5 February 1853, reprinted in Slater 1994/1996/1998:III (1998), 114.
5 Charles Dickens, *Pickwick Papers* ch. 33.
6 Thackeray 1898:302.
7 Woolf 1925:214.
8 Michael Ignatieff, interviewed on BBC programme *Private passions*, January 1997.
9 Belloc 1954/1991:152.
10 *Concise Oxford Dictionary*, 7th edition (1982).
11 Pope 1998:55.
12 John Carey 1987:xxxvi.

13 Chapter 4, p. 59.

14 S. Johnson 1775/1996:102.

15 John Carey 1987:xxxvi.

16 Hunter S. Thompson in Raymond 1993:22–3. According to Raymond, this comment was written in 1977, though not published till 1990.

17 Adrian Mitchell, in Summerfield 1974:225.

18 Marr 2004/2005:116.

19 Kipling 1892/1994.

20 Kipling 1892/1994:159.

21 Kipling 1892/1994:163.

22 Lacey 1998.

23 Shreve 1991/1994:328.

24 Golding and Elliott 1979/1999:112.

25 C. P. Scott, *Manchester Guardian*, 5 May 1921, reprinted in Bromley and O'Malley 1997.

26 Berkowitz 1997b:497.

27 James Carey 1989/1999:367.

28 Stuart Hall *et al.* 1978/1999:249.

29 Maxine Carr, the partner of Ian Huntley.

30 R. Lakoff 2000, Hunt 1999.

31 Shoemaker 1991/1997:57.

32 Butler and Keith 1999:22–3.

33 Marr 2004/2005:373.

34 Alan Hamilton, Tony Dawe and Brian McArthur, *The Times*, 13 January 1993.

35 Frayn 1967/2000:6.

36 Frayn 1965/1995:61.

37 Frayn 1965/1995:61.

38 Frayn 1965/1995:62.

39 Frayn 1965/1995:30.

40 Finkel 2005. Reviewed by Brian Appleyard in the *Sunday Times*, 15 May 2005.

41 Paul Harris, *Observer*, 29 February 2004.

42 Paul Harris, *Observer*, 21 March 2004.

43 Paul Harris, *Observer*, 21 March 2004.

44 John Humphrys, *Sunday Times*, 8 January 2004.
45 Roth, quoted in introduction to Wolfe 1988/1990:xiii.
46 Wolfe 1988/1990:xxviii.
47 Morgan, quoted in Matt Wells, *Guardian*, 7 May 2004.
48 Morgan 2005:x.
49 John Carey 1987:xxxv.
50 John Carey 1987:xxxv.
51 David Lodge, 'My hols', *Sunday Times*, 4 September 2005.
52 Marr 2004/2005:106.
53 Adie 2002:1.
54 Adie 2002:363.
55 D. M. Lewis 2003.
56 Snoddy 2003:19.
57 *Observer*, 21 May 2006.
58 Schudson 1995:52.
59 Quoted in www.quotatio.com/m/miller-arthur-quotes.html.

REFERENCES

Adie, Kate (2002). *The kindness of strangers*. London: Headline.
Agard, John (1985). *Mangoes and bullets: selected and new poems*. London: Pluto Press.
Aitchison, James (1988). *Writing for the press*. London: Hutchinson.
Aitchison, Jean (1963). Homeric *ánthos*. *Glotta* 41, 271–7.
  (1964). Telamónios Aías and other patronymics. *Glotta* 42, 132–7.
  (1992). Good birds, better birds and amazing birds: the development of prototypes. In *Vocabulary and applied linguistics* edited by Henri Béjoint and Pierre Arnaud. London: Macmillan.
  (1994). 'Say, say it again Sam': the treatment of repetition in linguistics. In *Repetition* edited by Andreas Fischer. Tübingen: Gunter Narr, 15–34.
  (1996/2000). *The seeds of speech: language origin and evolution*. Cambridge: Cambridge University Press. (Canto edition 2000.)
  (1997). *The language web: the power and problem of words*. Cambridge: Cambridge University Press.
  (1998). *The articulate mammal: an introduction to psycholinguistics*. 4th edn. London: Routledge.
  (2001). *Language change: progress or decay?* 3rd edn. Cambridge: Cambridge University Press.

(2003a). From Armageddon to war: the language of terrorism. In Aitchison and Lewis (2003b).

(2003b). *Words in the mind*. 3rd edn. Oxford: Blackwell.

(2003c). Metaphors, models and language change. In *Motives for language change*. Edited by R. Hickey. Cambridge: Cambridge University Press.

(2003d). *Linguistics*. 6th edn. London: Hodder and Stoughton 'Teach Yourself'.

Aitchison, Jean and Lewis, Diana M. (2003a). Introduction. In Aitchison and Lewis (2003b).

(eds.) (2003b). *New media language*. London: Routledge.

Aitchison, Jean, Lewis, Diana M. and Naylor, Bronwyn (2000). CAR MURDER HUBBY CAGED – and other murderous headlines. *English Today* 16.1, 23–30.

Andrews, Robert (ed.) (1996). *Cassell dictionary of contemporary quotations*. London: Cassell.

Au, W. (1993). *The sonar of dolphins*. Berlin: Springer Verlag.

Auden, W. H. (1976). *Collected poems* edited by E. Mendelson. London: Faber and Faber.

Ayto, John (1990). *Bloomsbury dictionary of word origins*. London: Bloomsbury.

(1999). *Twentieth century words*. Oxford: Oxford University Press.

Bagnall, Nicholas (1993). *Newspaper language*. London: Focal.

Bailey, Richard W. (1992). *Images of English: a cultural history of the language*. Cambridge: Cambridge University Press.

Baxter, J. and Downing, M. (2001). *The day that shook the world: understanding September 11th*. London: BBC Worldwide.

Beekes, R. S. P. (1995). *Comparative Indo-European linguistics: an introduction*. Amsterdam: John Benjamins.

Bell, Allan (1991). *The language of news media*. Oxford: Blackwell.

Belloc, Hilaire (1954/1991). *Complete verse of Hilaire Belloc*. London: Pimlico.

Bellow, Saul (1961/2001). *Herzog*. London: Penguin.

Berkowitz, Dan (1997a). Epilogue: applying the tools to study news. In Berkowitz (1997b).

Berkowitz, Dan (ed.) (1997b). *Social meaning of news: a text-reader*. London: Sage.

Biber, Douglas (1988). *Variation across speech and writing*. Cambridge: Cambridge University Press.

(1995). *Dimensions of register variation: a cross-linguistic comparison*. Cambridge: Cambridge University Press.

(2003). Compressed noun-phrase structures in newspaper discourse: the competing demands of popularization vs. economy. In Aitchison and Lewis (2003b).

Biber, Douglas, Conrad, Susan and Reppen, Randi (1998). *Corpus linguistics: investigating language structure and use*. Cambridge: Cambridge University Press.

Biber, Douglas, Johansson, Stig, Leech, Geoffrey, Conrad, Susan and Finegan, Edward (1999). *Longman grammar of spoken and written English*. London: Longman.

Bolton, W. F. (1966). *The English language: essays by English and American men of letters 1490–1839*. Cambridge: Cambridge University Press.

Borges, Jorge Luis (1969/1974). *The book of imaginary beings*. London: Penguin.

Boyd, Andrew (1994). *Broadcast journalism: techniques of radio and TV news*. 3rd edn. Oxford: Focal Press.

Boyd-Barrett, Oliver and Newbold, Chris (eds.) (1999). *Approaches to media: a reader*. London: Arnold.

Bradford, Richard (1996a). Studying poetry. In Bradford (1996b).

(ed.) (1996b). *Introducing literary studies*. London: Prentice Hall / Harvester Wheatsheaf.

Brewer, E. C. (2005). *Brewers dictionary of phrase and fable*. 17th edn, revised by John Ayto. London: Cassell.

Bromley, Michael and O'Malley, Tom (1997). *A journalism reader*. London: Routledge.

Brown, Lesley (ed.) (1993). *The new shorter Oxford dictionary*. Oxford: Oxford University Press.

Bulwer-Lytton, Edward (1840/1953). *Money*. In *Nineteenth-century plays* edited by George Rowell. London: Oxford University Press, 47–120.

Burns, Lynette Sheridan (2002). *Understanding journalism*. London: Sage.

Butler, Michael and Keith, George (1999). *Language, power and identity*. London: Hodder and Stoughton.

Butterworth, Brian (1999). *The mathematical brain*. London: Macmillan.

Campanile, Enrico (1987). Indogermanische Dichtersprache. In *Studien zum indogermanischen Wortschatz* edited by W. Meid. Innsbrück: Innsbrucker Beiträge zur Sprachwissenschaft, 21–8.

Carey, James (1989/1999). Mass communication and cultural studies. In Boyd-Barrett and Newbold (1999).

Carey, John (ed.) (1987). *The Faber book of reportage*. London: Faber and Faber.

 (2005). *What good are the arts?* London: Faber and Faber.

Carney, E. (1994). *A survey of English spelling*. London: Routledge.

Carroll, Lewis (1939/1982). *The complete works of Lewis Carroll*. London: Penguin.

Chadwick, John (1958). *The decipherment of Linear B*. Cambridge: Cambridge University Press.

Chapman, Raymond (1984). *The treatment of sounds in language and literature*. Oxford: Blackwell.

 (1992). 'Ballad'. In *The Oxford companion to the English language* edited by Tom McArthur. Oxford: Oxford University Press.

Chappell, W. (1859/1965). *The ballad Literature and popular music of the olden time*, vols. I–II. London: Dover.

Child, Francis James (ed.) (1882–98/1965). *The English and Scottish popular ballads*, vols. I–V. New York: Dover.

Coe, Michael D. (1992/1994). *Breaking the Maya code*. London: Penguin.

Cohn, Carol (1987/1989). Nuclear language and how we learned to pat the bomb. In *Exploring language*. 5th edn, edited by Gary Goshgarian. Glenview, IL: Scott Foresman.

Coleridge, Samuel Taylor (1993). *Poems* edited by John Beer. London: Dent.

Coltheart, M., Patterson, K. E. and Marshall, J. C. (eds.) (1987). *Deep dyslexia.* 2nd edn. London: Routledge and Kegan Paul.

Conboy, Martin (2002). *The press and popular culture.* London: Sage.

(2004). *Journalism: a critical history.* London: Sage.

(2006). *Tabloid Britain: constructing a community through language.* London: Routledge.

Cook, G. (2001). *The discourse of advertising.* 2nd edn. London: Routledge.

Coppens, Yves (1994). East Side story: the origin of humankind. *Scientific American* 270.5, 62–79.

Cotter, C. (2001). Discourse and the media. In *The handbook of discourse analysis* edited by D. Schiffrin, D. Tannen and H. T. Hamilton. Oxford: Blackwell.

Coulmas, Florian (1996). *The Blackwell encyclopaedia of writing systems.* Oxford: Blackwell.

Crystal, David (1998). *Language play.* London: Penguin.

Crystal, David and Crystal, Hilary (2000). *Words on words: quotations about language and literature.* London: Penguin.

Crystal, David and Davy, Derek (1969). *Investigating English style.* London: Longman.

Curran, James and Seaton, Jean (2003). *Power without responsibility: the press, broadcasting, and new media in Britain.* 6th edn. London: Routledge.

de la Mare, Walter (1913/1955). *Peacock pie: a book of rhymes.* London: Faber and Faber.

Derrida, Jacques (1967/1997). *Of grammatology.* Translated by G. C. Spivak. Baltimore and London: The Johns Hopkins University Press.

De Waal, Frans B. M. (2005). How animals do business. *Scientific American* 292.4, 55–61.

Diringer, David (1962). *Writing.* London: Thames and Hudson.

(1968). *The alphabet: a key to the history of mankind.* London: Hutchinson.

Doyle, Sir Arthur Conan (1892/1981). The adventure of the blue carbuncle. In *Adventures of Sherlock Holmes* (1892) in *The Complete Sherlock Holmes.* London: Penguin.

Dukes, J. A. (2002). Spelling reform. *Oxford Magazine* (Noughth Week, Trinity Term), 3–4.

Dunn, Douglas (1986). *Selected poems 1964–1983*. London: Faber and Faber.

Elgin, Susan H. (1993). *Genderspeak: men, women and the gentle art of verbal self-defense*. New York: Wiley.

Eliot, T. S. (1949). *Four quartets*. London: Faber.

Ellis, Alexander John (1845). *A plea for phonotypy and phonography, or, speech-printing and speech-writing*. Bath: Pitman.

Elman, Jeffrey L., Bates, Elizabeth A., Johnson, Mark H., Karmiloff-Smith, Annette, Parisi, Domenico and Plunkett, Kim (1996). *Rethinking innateness: a connectionist perspective on development*. Cambridge, MA: MIT Press.

Engel, Matthew (1996). *Tickle the public: one hundred years of the popular press*. London: Gollancz.

Evans, Harold (2000). *Essential English for journalists, editors and writers*. Revised edn. London: Pimlico.

Fedler, Fred, Bender, John R., Davenport, Lucinda and Drager, Michael W. (2001). *Reporting for the media*. 7th edn. New York: Harcourt.

Fenton, James (2002). *An introduction to English poetry*. London: Viking.

Finkel, Michael (2005). *True story: murder, memoir, mea culpa*. London: Chatto.

Frayn, Michael (1965/1995). *The tin men*. London: Penguin. (1967/2000). *Towards the end of the morning*. London: Penguin.

Frost, Robert (1971). *The poetry of Robert Frost* edited by E. C. Lathem. London: Jonathan Cape.

Furniss, Tom and Bath, Michael (1996). *Reading poetry: an introduction*. London: Longman.

Galtung, Johan and Ruge, Mari Holmboe (1965/1999). The structure of foreign news. *Journal of Peace Research* 2.1, 61–91. Reprinted in Tumber (1999).

Gavins, Joanna and Steen, Gerard (2003). *Cognitive poetics in practice*. London: Routledge.

Geeraerts, Dirk (1989). Prospects and problems of prototype theory. *Linguistics* 27, 587–612.

Gelb, Ignace J. (1963). *A study of writing*. 2nd edn. Chicago: University of Chicago Press.

Gibbs, Raymond. W. (1994). *The poetics of mind: figurative thought, language and understanding*. Cambridge: Cambridge University Press.

Gleitman, L. R., Gleitman, H. and Shipley, E. F. (1972). The emergence of the child as grammarian. *Cognition* 1, 137–64.

Goatly, Andrew (1997). *The language of metaphors*. London: Routledge.

Golding, Peter and Elliott, Philip (1979/1999). Making the news. In Tumber (1999).

Goldsmith, Oliver (1762/1970). *The citizen of the world*. London: Dent.

Goodall, J. (1986). *The chimpanzees of Gombe: patterns of behavior*. Cambridge, MA: Harvard University Press.

Graddol, David and Boyd-Barrett, Oliver (1994). *Media texts: authors and readers*. Clevedon: Multilingual Matters.

Grant, James (1871). *The newspaper press: its origin – progress – and present position*, vol. II. London: Tinsley.

Gray, Alasdair (2000). *The book of prefaces*. London: Bloomsbury.

Greenslade, Roy (2003/2004). *Press gang: how newspapers make profits from propaganda*. London: Pan.

Griffiths, Dennis (2006). *Fleet Street: five hundred years of the press*. London: The British Library.

Griggs, Earl Leslie (ed.) (1956–71/2000). *The collected letters of Samuel Taylor Coleridge*, vols. I–VI. Oxford: Clarendon Press. (Reprint 2000, Oxford University Press.)

Haiman, J. (1985). *Natural syntax: iconicity and erosion*. Cambridge: Cambridge University Press.

Hall, Stuart, Critcher, Chas, Jefferson, Tony, Clarke, John and Roberts, Brian (1978/1999). Policing the crisis. In Tumber (1999).

Halliday, F. (2002). *Two hours that shook the world. September 11, 2001: causes and consequences*. London: Saqi Books.

Halliday, M. A. K. (1994). A note on the grammar of little texts. In *An approach to functional grammar*. 2nd edn. London: Arnold.

Hanna, P. R., Hanna, J. S., Hodges, R. E. and Rudorf, E. H. (1966). *Phoneme–grapheme correspondences as clues to spelling improvement*. Washington DC: US Department of Health, Education and Welfare.

Harcup, Tony (2004). *Journalism: principles and practice*. London: Sage.

Heaney, Seamus (1990). *New selected poems 1966–1987*. London: Faber and Faber.

Herbert, A. P. (1931). *A book of ballads: the collected light verse of A. P. Herbert*. London: Ernest Benn.

Hock, H. H. and Joseph, B. D. (1996). *Language history, language change, and language relationship*. Berlin: Mouton de Gruyter.

Hockett, Charles F. (1958). *A course in modern linguistics*. New York: Macmillan.

Holroyd, Michael (1991). *Bernard Shaw*, vol. III. London: Chatto and Windus.

Home Office (1992). *Criminal statistics. England and Wales*. London: HMSO.

Horrie, Chris (2003). *Tabloid nation: from the birth of the Daily Mirror to the death of the tabloid*. London: Deutsch.

Hughes, John P. (1994). Languages and writing. In *Language: introductory readings*. 5th edn, edited by Virginia P. Clark, Paul A. Escholz and Alfred F. Rosa. New York: St Martins Press, 664–81.

Hughes, Ted (1957). *The hawk in the rain*. London: Faber and Faber.

Hughes, Ted (1960). *Lupercal*. London: Faber and Faber.

Humboldt, Wilhelm von (1836/1988). *On language: the diversity of human language-structure and its influence on the mental development of mankind*. Translated by Peter Heath. Cambridge: Cambridge University Press.

Hunt, Darnell M. (1999). *O. J. Simpson facts and fictions: news rituals in the construction of reality*. Cambridge: Cambridge University Press.

Jackendoff, Ray (1999). Possible stages in the evolution of language. *Trends in the Cognitive Sciences* 3.7, 272–9.

(2002). *Foundations of language: brain, meaning, grammar, evolution*. Oxford: Oxford University Press.

Jakobson, Roman (1958/1996). Closing statement: linguistics and poetics. In Weber (1996).

Jennings, Elizabeth (1989). *Tributes*. Manchester: Carcanet Press.

John, Andrew with Blake, Stephen (2001). *The total txtmsg dictionary*. London: Michael O'Mara.

Johnson, Mark (1987). *The body in the mind: the bodily basis of meaning, imagination and reason*. Chicago: University of Chicago Press.

Johnson, Samuel (1755/1990). *A dictionary of the English language*. London: Longman.

Johnson, Samuel (1775/1996). A journey to the Western Islands of Scotland. In *Journey to the Hebrides* edited by Ian McGowan. Edinburgh: Canongate.

Jonson, Ben (1631/1988). *The staple of news* edited by Anthony Parr. Manchester: Manchester University Press.

Karmiloff-Smith, Annette (1992). *Beyond modularity: a developmental perspective on cognitive science*. Cambridge, MA: MIT Press.

Keats, John (1908). *The poetical works of John Keats* edited by H. Buxton Forman. Oxford: Oxford University Press.

Keegan, Paul (ed.) (2000/2001). *The new Penguin book of English verse*. London: Penguin.

Kipling, Rudyard (1892/1994). A matter of taste. In *The Oxford book of sea stories* edited by Tony Tanner. Oxford: Oxford University Press.

(1940). *The definitive edition of Rudyard Kipling's verse*. London: Hodder and Stoughton.

Kirk, G. S. (1985). *The Iliad: a commentary*. Cambridge: Cambridge University Press.

Kittay, Eva F. (1987). *Metaphor: its cognitive and linguistic structure*. Oxford: Clarendon.

Klima, Edward S. and Bellugi, Ursula (1979). *The signs of language*. Cambridge, MA: Harvard University Press.

Kniffka, H. (1980). *Soziolinguistik und empirische Textanalyse: Schlagzeiten und Leadformulierung in amerikanischen Tageszeitungen*. Tübingen: Niemeyer.

Knowles, Frank. (1996). Lexicographical aspects of health metaphors in financial text. *Proceedings of EURALEX 96* Gothenburg University, 789–96.

Koestler, Arthur (1978). *Janus: a summing up*. London: Hutchinson.

Kövesces, Z. (1988). *The language of love*. London and Toronto: Associated University Presses.

(2000). *Metaphor and emotion: language, culture, and body in human feeling*. Cambridge: Cambridge University Press.

(2002). *Metaphor: a practical introduction*. Oxford: Oxford University Press.

Kyle, J. G. and Woll, Bencie (1985). *Sign language: the study of deaf people and their language*. Cambridge: Cambridge University Press.

Lacey, Nick (1998). *Image and representation: key concepts in media studies*. London: Palgrave.

Lakoff, George (1987). *Women, fire and dangerous things*. Chicago: University of Chicago Press.

Lakoff, George and Johnson, Mark (1980). *Metaphors we live by*. Chicago: University of Chicago Press.

Lakoff, George and Turner, Mark (1989). *More than cool reason: a field guide to poetic metaphor*. Chicago: University of Chicago Press.

Lakoff, Robin (2000). *The language war*. Berkeley: University of California Press.

Lamb, Charles (1833/n.d.). Elia: newspapers thirty-five years ago. In *The essays of Elia*. London: Nelson.

La Mettrie, Julien Offray de (1748/1912). *Man a machine*. La Salle, IL: Open Court.

Lane, H. (ed.) (1984). *The deaf experience: classics in language and education*. Translated by Franklin Philip. Cambridge, MA: Harvard University Press.

Larkin, Philip (ed.) (1973). *The Oxford book of twentieth-century English verse*. Oxford: Oxford University Press.

Lear, Edward (1871/1994). *Complete nonsense*. Ware, Herts.: Wordsworth.

Lewis, Diana M. (2003). Online news: a new genre? In Aitchison and Lewis (2003b).

Lewis, Jon E. (ed.) (2003). *The mammoth book of journalism*. London: Robinson.

Lloyd, A. L. (1967). *Folk song in England*. London: Lawrence and Wishart.

Lord, Albert B. (1960/2000). *The singer of tales*. 2nd edn, edited by Stephen Mitchell and Gregory Nagy. Cambridge, MA: Harvard University Press.

The Lutheran hymnal (1941). St Louis, MO: Concordia Publishing House.

Lyons, John (1968). *Introduction to theoretical linguistics*. Cambridge: Cambridge University Press.

Mac Cormac, Earl R. (1985). *A cognitive theory of metaphor*. Cambridge, MA: MIT Press.

Mallory, J. P. (1989). *In search of the Indo-Europeans: language, archaeology and myth*. London: Thames and Hudson.

Mardh, Ingrid (1980). *Headlinese: on the grammar of English front page headlines*. Lund: CWK Gleerup.

Marr, Andrew (2004/2005). *My trade: a short history of British journalism*. London: Pan.

Marshack, A. (1991). *The roots of civilization*. 2nd edn. London: Moyer Bell.

Marshall, John (1976). Neuropsychological aspects of orthographic representation. In *New approaches to language mechanisms* edited by R. J. Wales and Edward Walker. Amsterdam: North-Holland.

Masefield, John (1984/1988). *Selected poems*, selected by Donald E. Stanford. Manchester: Carcanet Press.

McGough, Roger (1989/1990). *Blazing fruit: selected poems 1967–1987*. London: Penguin.

Mellars, P. (1993). Archaeology and modern human origins in Europe. *Proceedings of the British Academy* 82, 1–35.

Mills, Eleanor and Cochrane, Kira (eds.) (2005). *Cupcakes and Kalashnikovs: 100 years of the best journalism by women.* London: Constable.

Milne, A. A (1926/1978). *Winnie-the-Pooh.* London: Methuen.

Morgan, Piers (2005). *The insider: the private diaries of a scandalous decade.* London: Ebury Press.

Myers, Greg (1994). *Words in ads.* London: Arnold.

(1999). *Ad-worlds: brands, media, audiences.* London: Arnold.

Nänny, M. and Fischer, O. (eds.) (1999). *Form miming meaning: iconicity in language and literature.* Amsterdam: John Benjamins.

Nash, Ogden (1985). *Candy is dandy: the best of Ogden Nash,* selected by Linell Smith and Isabel Eberstadt. London: Methuen.

Nevinson, Henry W. (1925). A farewell to Fleet Street. In *Selected modern English essays* edited by Geoffrey Cumberlege. Oxford: Oxford University Press.

Ni, Yibin (2003). Noun phrases in media texts: a quantificational approach. In Aitchison and Lewis (2003b).

Nottebohm, F. (1975). A zoologist's view of some language phenomena with particular emphasis on vocal learning. In *Foundations of language development,* vol. I, edited by E. H. Lenneberg and E. Lenneberg. New York: Academic Press.

O'Connell, Sheila (1999). *The popular print in England.* London: The British Museum Press.

Ong, Walter J. (1988/2002). *Orality and literacy.* London: Routledge.

Opie, Iona and Opie, Peter (1951/1997). *The Oxford dictionary of nursery rhymes.* Oxford: Oxford University Press.

Ortony, Andrew (1993). *Metaphor and thought.* 2nd edn. Cambridge: Cambridge University Press.

Orwell, George (1946/1962). Politics and the English language. In *Inside the whale and other essays.* London: Penguin, 143–56.

Palmer, Michael (1978). The British press and international news, 1851–99. In *Newspaper history* edited by G. Boyce, J. Curran and P. Wingate. London: Constable.

Parris, Matthew (ed.) (1994). *Scorn*. London: Hamish Hamilton.

Parry, Milman (1930/1971). *The making of Homeric verse: the collected papers of Milman Parry* edited by Adam Parry. Oxford: Clarendon Press.

Paulin, Tom (1999). *The wind dog*. London: Faber and Faber.

Philip, Neil (ed.) (1996). *The new Oxford book of children's verse*. Oxford: Oxford University Press.

Pinker, Steven (1994). *The language instinct: the new science of language and mind*. London: Allen Lane, The Penguin Press.

Pope, Rob (1998). Introduction to English studies. In *The English studies book* edited by R. Pope. London: Routledge.

Preston, John (1999/2000). *Ink*. London: Black Swan.

Puttenham, George (1589/1970). *The arte of English poesy*. 2nd edn, edited by D. G. Willcock and A. Walker. Cambridge: Cambridge University Press.

Raine, Craig (2000). *Collected poems 1978–1999*. London: Picador.

Randall, David (2005). *The great reporters*. London: Pluto.

Raymond, Joad (ed.) (1993). *Making the news: an anthology of the newsbooks of revolutionary England, 1641–1660*. Moreton-in-Marsh, Gloucs.: The Windrush Press.

Reddy, Michael (1979/1993). The conduit metaphor: a case of frame conflict in our language about language. In Ortony (1993).

Rée, Jonathan (1999). *I see a voice: language, deafness and the senses – a philosophical history*. London: HarperCollins.

Rhodes, Richard (1994). Aural images. In *Sound symbolism* edited by L. Hinton, J. Nichols and J. J. Ohala. Cambridge: Cambridge University Press.

Richards, Ivor A. (1936). *The philosophy of rhetoric*. Oxford: Oxford University Press.

Roberts, Phil (2000). *How poetry works*. 2nd edn. London: Penguin.

Robinson, Andrew (1995). *The story of writing*. London: Thames and Hudson.

(2002). *The man who deciphered Linear B: the story of Michael Ventris*. London: Thames and Hudson.

Rollings, Andrew G. (2004). *The spelling patterns of English*. Munich: Lincom.

Rosch, Eleanor (1975). Cognitive representations of semantic categories. *Journal of Experimental Psychology: General* 104, 192–233.

Rowan, David (1998). *A glossary for the 90s*. London: Prion.

Sacks, Oliver (1989/1991). *Seeing voices: a journey into the world of the deaf*. London: Picador.

Sampson, Anthony (1996/1999). The crisis at the heart of our media. *British Journalism Review* 7.3, 42–51. Reprinted in Tumber (1999).

Saussure, Ferdinand de (1915/1959). *Cours de linguistique générale*. English translation by Wade Baskin: *Course in general linguistics*. New York: The Philosophical Library.

Schaller, Susan (1991). *A man without words*. Berkeley: University of California Press.

Schmandt-Besserat, Denise (1978/1986). The earliest precursor of writing. *Scientific American* 238.6, 50–9. Reprinted in *Language, writing and the computer: readings from the Scientific American*. (New York: Freeman).

(1992). *Before writing*. 2 vols. Austin: University of Texas Press.

Schneider, Kristina (2000). The emergence and development of headlines in English newspapers. In *English media texts past and present: language and textual structure* edited by Friedrich Ungerer. Amsterdam: John Benjamins, 45–66.

Schudson, Michael (1995). *The power of news*. Cambridge, MA: Harvard University Press.

Shaaber, Matthias A. (1929). *Some forerunners of the newspaper in England 1476-1622*. Philadelphia: University of Pennsylvania Press.

Shaw, Irwin (1977). *Beggarman, thief.* New York: Delacorte Press.

Shepherd, Leslie (1962). *The broadside ballad: a study in origins and meaning.* London: Herbert Jenkins.

(1969). *John Pitts: ballad printer of Seven Dials, London 1765–1844.* London: Private Libraries Association.

Sheridan, Richard Brinsley (1988). *The school for scandal and other plays* edited by Eric Rump. London: Penguin.

Sherrin, Ned (2001). *The Oxford dictionary of humorous quotations.* 2nd edn. Oxford: Oxford University Press.

Shoemaker, Pamela (1991/1997). A new gatekeeping model. In Berkowitz 1997b.

Shreve, Anita (1991/1994). *Strange fits of passion.* London: Abacus.

Silcock, Arnold (ed.) (1952). *Verse and worse: a private collection.* London: Faber and Faber, 1952.

Simon-Vandenbergen, Anne-Marie M. (1981). *The grammar of headlines in The Times.* Brussels: Koninklijke Academie voor Wetenschappen, Letteren en Schone Kunsten van België.

Simpson, Paul (2004). *Stylistics: a resource book for students.* London: Routledge.

Slater, Michael (ed.) (1994/1996/1998). *Dickens' journalism*, vols. I–III. London: Dent.

Smith, M. K., Pollio, H. R. and Pitts, M. K. (1981). Metaphor as intellectual history: conceptual categories underlying figurative usage in American English from 1675–1975. *Linguistics* 19, 911–35.

Snoddy, Raymond (1992). *The good, the bad and the unacceptable: the hard news about the British press.* London: Faber and Faber.

(2003). Modern media myths. In Aitchison and Lewis (2003b).

Snowling, Margaret (1987). *Dyslexia: a cognitive developmental perspective.* Oxford: Blackwell.

Sommerville, C. John (1996). *The news revolution in England: cultural dynamics of daily information.* Oxford: Oxford University Press.

Steen, Gerard (1994). *Understanding metaphor in literature*. London: Longman.

Stockwell, Peter (2002). *Cognitive poetics: an introduction*. London: Routledge.

Sugden, Philip (1995). *The complete history of Jack the Ripper*. London: Robinson.

Summerfield, Geoffrey (ed.) (1974). *Seven modern poets*. London: Penguin.

Swan, Michael (1995). *Practical English usage*. 2nd edn. Oxford: Oxford University Press.

Swift, Jonathan (1712). *A proposal for correcting, improving, and ascertaining the English tongue*. Reprinted in Bolton (1966).

Tanaka, Keiko (1994). *Advertising language: a pragmatic approach to advertisements in Britain and Japan*. London: Routledge.

Tannen, Deborah (1989). *Talking voices: repetition, dialogue, and imagery in conversational discourse*. Cambridge: Cambridge University Press.

Taylor, S. J. (1991). *Shock! Horror! The tabloids in action*. London: Bantam.

Thackeray, William Makepeace (1898). *The history of Pendennis*. London: Smith, Elder and Co.

Thième, P. (1964). The comparative method for reconstruction in linguistics. In *Language in culture and society* edited by D. Hymes. New York: Harper and Row.

Thomas, R. S. (2000). *Residues* edited by M. Wynn Thomas. Tarsett, Northumberland: Bloodaxe Books.

Trench, Richard Chenevix (1855). *On the study of words*. 6th edn. London: J. W. Parker.

  (1856). *English past and present*. 3rd edn, revised. London: Parker.

Trim, Richard (1998). How universal is metaphor? The case of drugs in European languages. *Lexicology* 244–70.

Tumber, Howard (ed.) (1999). *News: a reader*. Oxford: Oxford University Press.

van Dijk, Teun A. (1988). *News as discourse*. Hillsdale, NJ: Lawrence Erlbaum.

Vestergaard, Torben and Schröder, Kim (1985). *The language of advertising*. Oxford: Blackwell.

Watkins, Calvert (1995). *How to kill a dragon: aspects of Indo-European poetics*. Oxford: Oxford University Press.

Watt, Tessa (1991). *Cheap print and popular piety, 1550–1640*. Cambridge: Cambridge University Press.

Waugh, Evelyn (1930/1938). *Vile bodies*. London: Chapman & Hall, 1930 / Penguin, 1938.

(1938/1943). *Scoop*. London: Penguin.

Weber, Jean Jacques (ed.) (1996). *The stylistics reader: from Roman Jakobson to the present*. London: Arnold.

West, Martin (1988). The rise of the Greek epic. *Journal of Hellenic Studies* 108, 151–72.

Wilbur, Richard (1973). *Opposites*. New York: Harcourt Brace Jovanovich.

(2005). *Collected poems 1943–2004*. New York: Harcourt Brace.

Wilkes, Roger (2002). *Scandal: a scurrilous history of gossip*. London: Atlantic.

Williams, William Carlos (1988). *Collected poems Volume II 1939–1962* edited by Christopher MacGowan. Manchester: Carcanet, 1988.

Wolfe, Tom (1988/1990). *The bonfire of the vanities*. London: Picador.

Woolf, Virginia (1925). *The common reader*. London: Hogarth Press.

Yeats, William Butler (1990). *Collected poems*. London: Picador.

INDEX